Learner autonomy:
new insights

Autonomie de l'apprenant:
nouvelles pistes

Edited by Leni Dam

Sous la direction de Leni Dam

Association Internationale de
Linguistique Appliquée

AILA

International Association of
Applied Linguistic

AILA Review 15

ISSN 1461-0213

This issue of AILA is also available as a single book item published by Catchline on behalf of AILA, and distributed by Catchline. Catchline is a trading name of The English Company (UK) Ltd.

ISBN 1-902985-08-7

Production by Catchline
Typeset in Bembo 10/12
Cover design by Catchline

Printed in the United Kingdom
by The Charlesworth Group, Huddersfield, West Yorkshire

The AILA Review 15

The AILA Review is a publication of the Association Internationale de Linguistique Appliquée, an international federation of national associations for applied linguistics. AILA promotes, co-ordinates, and disseminates research, and collaborates with international non-governmental organisations in key areas of applied linguistics. AILA has affiliated associations and organisations in 35 countries.

La Revue de l'AILA est publiée par l'Association Internationale de Linguistique Appliquée, fédération d'associations nationales de linguistique appliquée. L'AILA promeut et coordonne la recherche, en dissémine les résultats, et collabore avec les organisations non-gouvernementales internationales dans les domaines essentiels de la linguistique appliquée. L'AILA a des associations qui lui sont affiliées dans 35 pays.

AMERICAN ASSOCIATION FOR APPLIED LINGUISTICS

BUSINESS OFFICE
AAAL
P. O. Box 361806
Birmingham, AL 35236
(205) 824-7700 Fax: (205) 823-2760
aaaloffice@aaal.org
www.aaal.org

EXECUTIVE COMMITTEE 2002-2003
President
MARGIE BERNS
Purdue University
English Department
Heavilon Hall
West Lafayette, IN 47907-1356
(765) 494-3769 Fax: (765) 494-3780
berns@purdue.edu

First Vice President
RICHARD SCHMIDT
University of Hawai'i
Dept. of Second Language Studies
1890 East-West Road
Honolulu, HI 96822
(808) 956-2784 Fax: (808) 956-2802
schmidt@hawaii.edu

Second Vice President
JAMES P. LANTOLF
The Pennsylvania State University
Center for Language Acquisition
304 Sparks Building
University Park, PA 16802
jpl7@psu.edu

Secretary-Treasurer
JOAN KELLY HALL
University of Georgia
Department of Language Education
125 Aderhold Hall
Athens, GA 30602
(706)542-4525 Fax: (706) 542-4509
jkhall@arches.uga.edu

Past President
WILLIAM GRABE
Northern Arizona University
English Department; Box 6032
Flagstaff, AZ 86011
(928) 523-6274 Fax: (928) 523-7074
william.grabe@nau.edu

Members-at-Large
ALISTER CUMMING
Ontario Institute for Studies in
Education of the University of Toronto

PATRICIA DUFF
University of British Columbia

NANCY HORNBERGER
University of Pennsylvania

Ex-Officio
DONNA CHRISTIAN
President, Center for Applied Linguistics

Newsletter Editor
SUSAN GONZO
University of Illinois
Division of English as an
International Language
3070 FLB
707 South Matthews Avenue
Urbana, IL 61801
s-gonzo@uiuc.edu

July 2002

Dear AAAL Member,

Enclosed is your copy of *AILA Review 15*. Each year AILA publishes a collection of articles on subjects of current interest in the field language studies. This year's topic, learner autonomy, has been increasingly represented on the program of both AAAL and the upcoming AILA Congress.

The volume comes to you as a benefit of membership in the American Association for Applied Linguistics.

It's a pleasure to be sending it off to you.

Best wishes,

Margie Berns

Margie Berns
AAAL President

Contents • Contenu

Introduction

Under the open title 'Promoting Learner Autonomy: new insights' papers for the 3rd symposium under the Scientific Commission on Learner Autonomy were called for. The symposium had three principal aims: first to arrange a programme of interest to experienced and novice practitioners and researchers in the field. Second, to gather as many people as possible who are working with the concept of learner autonomy (in practice as well as in theory), both to share and clarify interpretations, and to support and build practical and research initiatives. And third, to continue – if possible – from where we left off at the Aila Congress in Jyväskylä, Finland in 1996.

The incoming proposals clustered around three main headings which formed the programme of the symposium, and form the contents of this AILA *Review*: Dimensions of learner counselling; Assessment of processes and outcomes; Contexts and constraints when developing learner autonomy.

There were many strong papers to choose from – and the final collection indeed covered 'new insights' from various parts of the world. One of the presenters, Beverly Ann Carter, received one of the ten Solidarity Awards given by AILA 'to outstanding established or promising new scholars to ensure their participation in the 1999 AILA congress.'

As early as February 1999 the Scientific Commission was invited to submit papers from the 1999 Symposium on Learner Autonomy for publication in the AILA *Review*. It was agreed that this was a great opportunity both for the Commission and for the presenters. We can include only a selection of the papers submitted, but this volume has managed to include most papers from the symposium.

Under 'Dimensions of learner counselling' are the papers by David Crabbe, Alison Hoffmann, Sara Cotterall; by Richard Pemberton, Sarah Toogood, Susanna Ho, Jacqueline Lam; and by Beverly Ann Carter. The section 'Assessment of processes and outcomes' is represented by Jose Lai; by Marie-France Champagne, Terry Clayton, Nicholas Dimmitt, Matthew Laszewski, William Savage, Jonathan Shaw, Richmond Stroupe, Myint Myint Thein, Pierre Walter; and by Lienhard Legenhausen. Finally, Richard Smith and Naoko Aoki report their personal experiences with promoting learner autonomy in Japan in the section 'Contexts and constraints when developing learner autonomy'.

Promoting learner autonomy cannot take place only by reading about it – it has to be tried out. This selection of papers gives an insight into various steps taken by people from around the world. It is my hope that their experience will result in fuelling a growing interest in the development of learner autonomy. ▨

Leni Dam

◆ Examining the discourse of learner advisory sessions

◆ Le discours des séances de tutorat

David Crabbe, Alison Hoffmann, Sara Cotterall
Victoria University of Wellington, New Zealand

Abstract

The intention of this paper is to explore problems described by learners of a second language at university level. An understanding of the range of experiences that learners report in given learning contexts is likely to shed light on ways in which those learning contexts might be structured for better learning opportunities, or ways in which learners themselves might develop better strategies for making use of the opportunities that are already there. For example, one of the problem types identified in our data is a lack of fit between a learner's long-term language-learning goals and the immediate goals of the course they are enrolled in. The lack of fit could be dealt with through a modification of the curriculum design or by an increased understanding by the learner of how to manage the differing expectations. In either case, some intervention in the status quo of a particular context would be indicated. The problem descriptions were gathered through a series of interviews between individual learners and a language advisor. In order to focus our exploration of the problems, we began with three broad questions: In what way are the problems framed through the process of the interview itself? What learning goals are explicitly or implicitly set by or for the learner? What underlying learner beliefs about language learning emerge from the interviews? The paper concludes by proposing a framework to use in managing and analysing dialogues about learning.

Résumé

L'objectif de cet article est d'explorer les problèmes décrits par les apprenants d'une langue étrangère au niveau universitaire. La connaissance de l'étendue des expériences rapportées dans des contextes donnés par les apprenants permettra vraisemblablement de montrer comment on peut structurer ces contextes d'apprentissage ou comment les apprenants eux-mêmes peuvent développer de meilleures stratégies pour tirer parti des occasions déjà existantes. Par exemple, un des problèmes-types identifiés dans les informations recueillies est un manque d'harmonisation entre les objectifs à long terme de l'apprenant et les objectifs immédiats du cours suivi. Pour pallier ce manque d'harmonisation, on pourrait modifier le programme, ou encore l'apprenant en langue pourrait apprendre à s'adapter pour concilier les différentes attentes. Dans tous les cas, un changement sera nécessaire. Pour recueillir les données, un conseiller a interrogé individuellement les apprenants. De façon à se concentrer sur l'étude des problèmes, on se pose tout d'abord trois questions d'ordre général: Comment la procédure d'entrevue elle-même sert-elle de cadre pour aborder les problèmes? Quels sont les objectifs d'apprentissage explicitement ou implicitement établis par ou pour l'apprenant? Qu'est-ce que l'entrevue montre en ce qui concerne les opinions sous-jacentes des apprenants sur l'apprentissage des langues? Un système pour mener et analyser les entrevues avec les apprenants en langue est proposé dans la conclusion de cet article.

Introduction

The intention of this paper is to explore and interpret the language learning task[1] as described by learners of a second language at university level. An understanding of how learners characterise and respond to the task of learning a language in a given context is likely to shed light on ways in which learning opportunities might be enhanced, whether by learners or teachers. For example, one of the issues identified in our data is a lack of fit between a learner's long-term language learning goals and the immediate goals of the course on which they are enrolled. The lack of fit could be dealt with through a modification of the curriculum design or by an increased understanding by the learner of how to reconcile the differing expectations. In either case, some intervention in the status quo would be indicated.

In this study, the learners' perspectives on the learning task were gathered through a series of interviews between individual learners and a language advisor. In order to focus our exploration of the learning task, we began with three broad questions:

- In what way is any task difficulty framed through the process of the interview itself?
- What learning goals are explicitly or implicitly set by or for the learner?

- What underlying learner beliefs about language learning emerge from the interviews?

These focus questions derive both from our own hunches about critical aspects of individual performance in managing the language learning task, and from cognition-based models of language learning. The interest in task representation derives from research which shows that finding a solution to a problem requires an accurate and specific representation of the problem[2] (Newell and Simon, 1972). Goal-setting is an established component of motivation theory (Locke and Latham, 1990; Dörnyei, 1998), and beliefs are well-established as underlying influences on action or inaction. These three aspects obviously interrelate: the commonality is that they are all concerned ultimately with learning that is managed by a hypothetical learner who has positive and productive beliefs about language and language learning, and who is able to represent his or her language learning task in a balanced and detailed way, for example, by setting goals that are realistic and effective motivators of learning.

This paper reports on three case studies drawn from a language advisory service at Victoria University of Wellington. Working from transcribed interviews, it presents excerpts that relate to the three questions above. The data is not intended to be a full representation of the language learners' experiences. At one level it shows the potential of dialogue about learning; at another level it offers some insight into the three dimensions of the management of language learning which we feel advisory dialogues can usefully explore. What action might be required in a particular case is likely to vary according to the age, sophistication and personality of the learners, as well as the roles they expect and are expected to play in formal education. Nonetheless, we feel that there are generalisations that can be made from this study, particularly concerning the potential of dialogues with learners about language learning and the ways in which such dialogue can be further understood.

Each of the following three sections reports on a dialogue with a separate learner. The first section demonstrates how a problem is framed through a learner-advisor dialogue, driven by the advisor's goal to get the learner to articulate task difficulty as specifically as possible. The following two sections explore two aspects of cognition that are likely to influence learners in the action they take: the goals that they are working towards, and the beliefs that underpin their focus of attention.

Framing the task

Generally, learners seek an advisory session because they have experienced in their language learning a difficulty that prevents them from performing successfully. They are not always able to analyse or articulate that difficulty. One of the aims of the interview is to help them to do so within a problem-solving framework. This section looks at one interview transcript and summarises the way in which a language learning problem unfolds through the learner-advisor discourse.

An advisor who engages in a dialogue to identify problems and solutions in language leaning is working with at least three assumptions. The first is that an accurate and helpful representation of the problem can be formulated collaboratively from the learner's own reported experience and judgement. The second is that a formulation of the problem will help the learner or the advisor to identify specific tactics that the learner will find personally feasible. The third is that the learner will be able to apply and evaluate those tactics successfully. This rather clinical problem-solution approach can only be seen as an initial framework for action that will be affected by a number of variables both personal and contextual.

The interview is with Clare[3] who is enrolled in a Spanish course. Clare had successfully studied French at school, completed a six-week 'crash course' in Spanish and then spent some time over the summer in South America where she 'picked up a bit of the easy kind of stuff'. She then enrolled in a university course in introductory Spanish, which she passed confidently, and so continued to her current course, a more advanced paper in Spanish language. Clare's opening statement of difficulty in the interview is:

> I'm like completely lost and I don't know what's happening and I mean I've been doing quite a bit of work but I just don't seem to be sort of taking it all in at all, like I've been trying to learn sort of the past tense and the imperfect and stuff and trying to take it in

She makes an unfavourable comparison with her previous, successful experience of learning French, a comparison that is repeated on several occasions. She expresses the belief that Spanish is not a difficult language and says that she is putting in a lot of effort but with no good result. The interviewer (also the writer of this section) takes a problem-solution orientation early in the interview:

> the key to these sorts of things... is... to try... to work out exactly what the problem is because different problems will lead to different solutions so it'd be good to think, to talk a bit about what's changed

This statement is clearly intended to steer the discourse into a pre-determined framework. The question is to what extent the intention was realised in this case. There is no space here to fully represent the unfolding discourse, but Table 1 (pages 8 and 9) shows a selection of learner statements from the first half of the interview with an indication of the role of the interviewer in prompting these statements.

The statements in Table 1 show to some extent how the problem representation is built up, prompted by the interviewer but building on the perceptions of the learner. The initial statement of the learning problem as not being able to 'take things in' is developed into a fuller statement that includes a performance dimension (not being able to express herself), a language control dimension (grammatical patterns and vocabulary) and finally an affective dimension (being a weaker member of the class). This fuller (but by no means full) representation of the problem, together with the three general tactics suggested by Clare, sets a base of shared understanding from which specific tactics are discussed in the second half of the interview (not represented here).

Table 1 Statements of problem as they appeared in the discourse

Interviewer's prompts	Clare's statements of problem	Learning tactics raised by Clare
	I think everything seems to be going a lot faster we've had a lot of people join the class now who obviously learnt Spanish before and a lot of them are even finding it boring you know they've learnt all this kind of stuff [ ] I feel after [the introductory course] we don't know enough	
	when I learnt French at school I guess there was a lot more interaction I mean I never thought about it before I took the subject but of course it's incredibly hard learning a language in a lecture theatre it's like you know somebody talking at you rather than you actually having a chance to do it yourself	maybe I just need more time to actually practise it like I was reading the thing out there about sort of videos and tapes and stuff there are maybe I just need to come down here and do some of that kind of stuff
	but I'm sure yeah I just not it just doesn't seem to stick so much anymore	
	with our a-v classes we have like on a Thursday morning I'm finding now everybody can express their ideas more than I can [ ] if I'm talking to people I can't express what I'm trying to say	
when you feel you can't express your ideas what do you think it is that you don't have that would enable you to express these ideas	I just I can't think quick enough to be able to I mean first of all I'm thinking in English which is you know something you shouldn't do obviously but um I don't feel I know enough vocabulary I don't feel I know my tenses or my verbs I don't feel I know anything enough [ ] to be able to try and construct a sentence out of it accurately	
and yet you did that in South America presumably	yeah I guess over there I just you know... I wouldn't know the verb but people would understand you if you just sort of said [ ] people would seem to understand that but [ ] here of course we need to actually know the grammar and stuff [ ] I just seem to know enough to be able to I mean when like when someone talks at me in Spanish they can talk for half an hour and I'll understand it [ ] I just can't seem to respond to it	

Table 1 continued

Interviewer's prompts	Clare's statements of problem	Learning tactics raised by Clare
okay [ ] let's go back to the expression thing [ ] when you hesitate because you haven't the Spanish flowing out as it were, what is it you're looking for? – is it the vocabulary or [ ] are you hesitating because of the grammatical structure	generally grammatical structure [ ] 'cause if it's vocabulary [ ] I'll know some way to get around it if I don't know the exact word I'll know another word that's similar so yeah it's pretty much the grammar I mean like we're doing a lot of past and imperfect now and I just can't think it fast enough to be able to express it	
[ ] okay so [ ] where does the solution lie, do you think		um I don't know I guess just I just learn the grammar so that I know it well enough to be able to say it [ ]
how much of it is a [ ] affective problem of [ ] not wanting to appear to be the one who knows least in the class for example [ ] is that an issue	yeah I mean I guess it is it's kind of I mean it's stops me from [ ] saying so much I mean I always remember at school in French I was always sort of you know the one in the class who did know everything and who could always answer the questions and stuff so now it's like okay so I'm not that	I was sort of was considering getting maybe a tutor or something so I had someone where it was just sort of one on one where I wasn't feeling worried about everything else where I could just yeah practise it and stuff
	the other day we started talking about how cold it was in Russia and whatever um things just yeah things just come up and I mean like in the um in the classes and stuff I mean I won't not say anything like if they ask me I won't say pass I mean I don't think that's gonna do me any good at all but I just won't stick up my hand and go ooh ooh I'll give it a go	
that's fair representation of the problem [ ] why don't I suggest one or two things that\ come to mind and you can you can tell if they're gonna work 'cause they're just from me [ ]		

The difficulty that Clare has expressed is in relation to the task of succeeding on the course rather than the bigger task of learning the language. It is hardly surprising that a personal motivation to learn a language is eclipsed temporarily by the need to pass a course. (It is easy for an advisor to overlook this and to be talking at cross-purposes about implicit goals.) Action to achieve the course tasks is likely, therefore, to be more strongly motivated than action relating to personal language learning goals that are to some extent independent of the course. The challenge is to develop a frame of action that integrates the learner's personal motivation and experience with the learning and learning outcomes prescribed by the course in which they are enrolled. It is a hallmark of autonomy that a learner remains in control of their own learning and uses available learning opportunities to serve their own goals. In the context of formal education, they may have two goals – to learn the language to a certain level of proficiency and to pass the course. It is easy for these goals to remain separate. The next section looks at a second case study that illustrates this point.

Clarifying goals

Goals are an important motivational force in language learning. In a recent state of the art paper on motivation in language learning, Dörnyei has explained why:

> [Goals] direct attention and effort towards goal-relevant activities at the expense of activities that are not relevant; they regulate effort expenditure; they encourage persistence until the goal is accomplished; they promote the search for relevant action plans or task strategies. (Dörnyei, 1998:120)

Language learners enrolled in a course will have greater control over their learning if they are clear about the nature of the goals of the language course while at the same time being clear about their own wider language learning goals. The two sets of objectives may not match closely, but ideally course goals should feed into long-term personal goals.

Any second-language learner has as an objective the development of fluency or accuracy or both. Stern (1990) has used the terms *analytic* and *experiential* as descriptors of these complementary aspects of the language learning task. An analytic learning focus is, according to Stern, essentially attention to accuracy. It is a:

> Focus on aspects of L2, including phonology, grammar, functions, discourse, sociolinguistics; cognitive study of language items (rules and regularities); practice or rehearsal of language items or skill aspects; attention to accuracy and error avoidance. (Stern, 1990:106)

An experiential focus, on the other hand, is essentially a focus on fluency. Stern defines it as a focus on:

> Substantive and motivated topic or theme; …purposeful activity …not exercises; language… [which] uses any of the four skills as part of purposeful action; …priority of meaning transfer and fluency over

linguistic error avoidance and accuracy. (Stern, 1990:106)

Balanced language development, as Skehan (1998) points out, requires an even mix of analytic and experiential language learning focus. Successful learners 'balance attention to form and meaning throughout their learning careers. Such learners switch attention judiciously' (1998:269). The reality is that most formal language learning situations focus on analytic, accuracy-focused activities, while naturalistic or immersion situations are experiential, with a high priority given to meaning transfer.

The following case-study data is taken from an advising session similar in format to the first. The learner's comments illustrate how the course has prompted her to move from a wider experiential focus in accord with her needs in daily life in a foreign country to a much narrower focus on achieving accuracy in the tasks of a course. A language advising interview has the potential to make such shifts of focus salient and to point out the need to maintain balance, if balanced language development is indeed the goal.

Nancy is a first-year university student enrolled in an introductory Italian language course. During the advisory session she reveals that she has spent time in Italy and learned Italian by living with an Italian family, interacting with native speakers in daily life and watching Italian television, and has developed a degree of fluency and confidence in interaction with Italian native speakers. Nancy has sought the advice of the language advisor (the writer of this section of the paper) because she is having difficulty meeting the demands of the Italian course for high levels of accuracy, in particular accuracy in matching sound to spelling when doing dictations. She starts by defining the reason for her visit:

> we were going to talk about dictations because I did one this morning [ ] and it went really well [ ] but you see what I did this morning which is not too bad 'cause I've been getting a lot more wrong

She then goes on to describe her problem in more detail:

> I did the first dictation and I got 3.2 out of 5 or something which you know is still a B [ ] so I practised and I did lots of dictations and I tried sounds and I tried to learn my vocab and we had a second dictation and I thought I'd done really well and I was really happy and I got it back and I got exactly the same sort of mark and I was like you know 'cause I've done so much work and I thought I was actually getting better

The interviewer attempts to move the focus from the learner's performance to the nature of the task by suggesting that it may have been a more difficult dictation, but Nancy feels it is her problem.

> I made so many little mistakes [ ] but then again [name of lecturer] says I should be able to hear the different sounds and even if I don't know the words I should be able to spell them

As the data shows, Nancy is concerned about the course requirement that she develop the ability to accurately match sound to written form, and her inability to meet this demand. In contrast she notes her earlier success in communicating despite not being able to spell accurately.

> I used to find it really easy in Italy listening to people talk, that's how I'd pick up the language if they had asked me to spell the words that they were saying there'd be no way I could probably say them quite well and probably get my point across

Nancy is working hard on accuracy in spelling and pronunciation, especially in relation to a new piece of assessment, a reading aloud test, which is about to take place.

> at the moment we are having an oral test and we have to prepare a dialogue – it's out of the book – and I've been going through and through trying to read out some of the words 'cause we have to learn them perfectly but some of them are quite difficult to say [ ] it's where to put the stress sometimes I get confused [ ] and I think I have a lot of problems with the /ye/ sound

Throughout the advising session there is a great deal of talk by the learner about the need for accuracy in spoken and written performance. She seems comfortable with the way the course goals have helped her to see aspects of her learning which she needs to work on.

> I still find that I say things um like I know the words and I know where they've gotta go but sometimes I pronounce them like my o's and my u's and my vowels a little bit like guarded I won't pronounce the o like enough [Interviewer: is that because you're unsure of whether it's an o or u do you think] it could have come from that (laughs) [ ] but I think the biggest problem is between a's and e's

The relevance of accuracy in speaking and writing can be understood in a university language course. But fluency is also an important component of language proficiency. At the end of the interview, in an attempt to bring experiential, fluency goals into focus, the advisor mentions the availability of Italian satellite television. At the mention of television Nancy comments on the role it played in her learning of Italian in Italy.

> oh I used to sit and watch TV in Italy all the time so even if I don't pick up things I usually can get the gist of the story [ ] I used to watch Baywatch and it's dubbed in Italian still I kept up with the story

After this reminiscence she switches the topic back to strategies for making vocabulary learning enjoyable (playing memory games, using coloured flip cards, and making vocabulary lists to put on the wall), and repeats an earlier point, namely that language learning at university is hard work and that she needs to motivate herself with these strategies as she has so much vocabulary to learn. So while Nancy may have begun to learn Italian with a desire to communicate in one form or other, her goals at university seem to have narrowed to meeting the demands of the course. It is hard to explain her current lack of interest in that enjoyable form of fluency practice, television watching, in any other way.

From one encounter with this learner it is not easy to judge whether her focus on accuracy is a short-term matter or a re-orientation in her thinking. To probe this and at the same time to foster autonomy in learners like Nancy, who are facing stringent and 'high-stakes' course demands, it may be helpful to make salient the value of both analytic and experiential activities in the language learning process. The advisor can achieve this not by undermining the value of the course objectives, but by encouraging an informed appreciation of the need to maintain this wider, more balanced focus. If learners are to manage the balance, they clearly need a schema of action in language learning that includes both components as an integrated approach to learning. Such an integration of fluency and accuracy work is underpinned by a productive set of beliefs about language and language learning. The next section attempts to show how the beliefs about language learning of one learner underpin the way he defines his problem, prioritises goals and selects strategies.

Identifying beliefs

The literature on cognitive development identifies two dimensions of metacognition – knowledge about cognition, and the regulation of cognition. Flavell (1987, cited in Wenden, 1998:517) suggests that beliefs about learning are a component of metacognitive knowledge. Metacognitive knowledge is generally classified into three categories, focusing on the learner, the learning task and the learning process. Flavell (1979) calls these three types of knowledge *person*, *task* and *strategic*. According to Wenden:

> person knowledge is general knowledge learners have acquired about human factors that facilitate or inhibit learning ... Task knowledge refers to what learners know about the purpose of a task ... the nature of a particular task ... a task's demands ... Strategic knowledge refers to general knowledge about what strategies are, why they are useful, and specific knowledge about when and how to use them. (Wenden, 1998:518)

In what follows, a number of beliefs about language learning, inferred from statements made by the learner, are discussed. In particular, his beliefs about the role of personal factors (person knowledge), the language learning demands of different situations and the role of competing goals (task knowledge), and the usefulness of various strategies (strategic knowledge) are explored.

This interview is with Igor, who, in contrast to the other interviewees, is a non-native speaker of English, and is not currently enrolled in a language course. He is a surgeon from Central Europe who is seeking registration as a doctor in New Zealand. He has attended three English language courses – two at the university – since arriving in New Zealand, but is now working independently on his English, principally by preparing to sit IELTS. Igor begins the interview by stating:

> um, now I recognise that I lose uh time by time my speaking skills yeah, because after finish my course in university I continue reading, continue listening study [ ] but I don't have good good environment

good possibilities for continue my speaking skills

Igor's initial statement of the 'problem' focuses on the affective dimension –
how to find a 'good environment' in which to practise his speaking skills, that
is, an environment which meets his personal needs. The language advisor (the
writer of this section of the paper) responds by suggesting a number of ways of
obtaining speaking practice. Most of these involve seeking interaction with
strangers in public settings. However Igor raises objections to these
suggestions, referring on a number of occasions to his emotional state (feeling
uncomfortable):

> yeah, yeah, but um this talking it's maybe unconvenient to speak with
> whisper like that, but if people hear that my English is not very good
> and ah maybe I look a little bit embarrassed

and his social role (study pressure, insufficient time):

> yeah but if I, if I um have um quite free time for my life, but now I feel
> a little bit uncomfortable for my situation here because I try to take my
> not my job but I try to study medical books and also now I study for
> IELTS test, so I don't have much time for … for finding places many
> places to speak

We can infer from these statements that Igor believes that people's reactions to
his spoken English can inhibit his efforts, and that the competing demands of
his long-term (medicine) and short-term (English language) goals make him
feel pressured, diverting energy from his language learning. However he
mentions two situations where he feels comfortable about speaking English –
meetings of local doctors, and meetings of the Theosophical Society. He
describes the Theosophical Society meetings in the following way:

> um, quite lucky about that because it's really really interesting topics for
> me [ ] and um, we have not very many people, we have like a small
> community, but everybody can go there and uh they are very friendly
> people and everybody can express personal idea with um very quiet
> environment and we have a tea time

Clearly this context meets Igor's criteria for a 'good environment… for
continue my speaking skills'. But what does he believe about the language
demands of taking part in such meetings? In both contexts, Igor is likely to be
exposed to discussion on familiar, demanding topics expressed in complex
language. He describes the issues discussed at the Theosophical Society as
'really really interesting', and cites 'cardiac surgery' and 'political question about
… humanitarian support' as topics discussed at the doctors' meetings. Igor
evidently finds it motivating and challenging to discuss such issues. He claims
to understand 'about 90%' of the discussion at the doctors' meetings, and
explains why attending is valuable:

> because it's um my practising understanding medical stuff

However, Igor's input and interaction in English appear to be biased towards a
focus on fluency where expressing meaning assumes priority (Skehan, 1998).

His interaction could also be said to favour cognitively demanding topics with familiar interlocutors who recognise and acknowledge his status. While this is highly logical in terms of establishing his professional identity, it is not likely to lead to balanced language development. When the advisor attempts to suggest that Igor obtain conversation practice by, for example, talking to strangers on public transport or chatting to staff in public offices, he displays little interest. The advisor then challenges him to analyse the type of input and interaction he needs most, by saying:

> well basically as a GP the most common thing you'll be doing all day every day is this sort of conversation sure you'll be saying where's the pain X, you know but you won't be talking technical language [ ] the most ordinary conversation is what will be your bread and butter as a GP do you understand what I mean

but Igor ignores the advisor's language-focused comment and explains:

> but I don't like to continue my work like a doctor in the GP area because if I could pass um general exams I after that I will try for study surgical skills

This leads us to consider the third area of Igor's beliefs – his goals. Throughout the interview, he talks about his study of English as a means to the end of being recognised as a doctor in New Zealand. Yet his conception of language learning appears somewhat naïve:

> but after when I finished my IELTS test, push out everything and concentrate on the medicine

Igor is so preoccupied with his ultimate goal of resuming work as a surgeon, that he appears to direct little effort to defining his language learning goals in more detail. Indeed, he is impatient to achieve his ends, and so states:

> yeah but ah maybe I want to get um very quickly very high skills about speaking

Yet he displays no ability to analyse what those speaking skills might involve in different situations or how they might develop, and the advisor's reaction which follows elicits no response:

> mm hmm I don't think that you can improve your speaking skills very quickly I don't think it's possible yeah

The final area of Igor's beliefs revealed in the interview relates to his strategic knowledge. He appears to believe in the usefulness of a number of strategies, reporting on both form-focused (analytic) activities, such as working with a teacher friend on dictation and writing tasks, and the meaning-focused (experiential) activities of attending meetings already discussed. Indeed the interview is motivated by his search for additional strategies to improve his speaking skills.

What the previous discussion suggests however, is that Igor's consideration of any strategies is filtered by his beliefs about personal factors, what constitute suitable topics and conversation partners, and relevance to his long-term goal.

Conclusion

What does this discussion suggest the three learners have in common, and what questions does it raise regarding the role and process of dialogue about learning? The main point to make about these learners is that they are all guided by a goal of some kind. To call the goal simply a language learning goal is, however, to miss an important point. The short-term goal for each of them is to pass a test and be accredited by an institution, even though their long-term goal might be to use the language effectively for real communication. The lack of integration of the long-term communication goal, the short-term assessment goal and the means of achieving them seems to be a productive aspect to explore. (It may even by a factor separating highly successful language learners from learners who struggle through courses.) If any generalisation at all can be made from only three case studies, it would be that goals occupy a central position in each of them. Making the goals explicit seems a useful basis for any subsequent discussion of strategic behaviour that might serve those goals.

Analysis of the dialogues suggests that an advisor needs to attend to at least three things (Table 2): first, unfold the problem; second, establish the learner's goals; and third, explore their beliefs about language learning. In an effective advisory session, each of these would be monitored by the advisor in an attempt both to prompt an elaborated statement of the learner's problem and goals, and to develop a discussion of relevant language learning beliefs. The immediate effectiveness of the session could be measured by how well the learners represent the problem, how committed they are to specific goals, and how aware they are of their beliefs about language learning.

It is relatively easy to prescribe a focus on goals and task difficulties and the beliefs underpinning choices that a learner might make. However, it is more problematic to be sure of whether the dialogue has prompted successful learning behaviour in the longer term. What would count as evidence that the dialogue had initiated change? Obviously a follow-up account is needed – ideally a longitudinal study of dialogue taking place over a longer period of time. Such a study would record what action had been taken by a learner and to what extent that action might have been prompted by dialogue (as opposed simply to further experience of language learning). Evidence of this might include learners' statements of new perceptions or appropriate learning activities, and later attribution of any subsequent action to the dialogue.

A final consideration is the context of the dialogue. In this case, the dialogue was one-to-one with an advisor and was initiated by learners who felt they had difficulties in achieving adequate performance. A learning dialogue can also take place between a teacher in an advisory role and a group of students: although the dynamic is different, the purpose and potential outcomes of the dialogue are the same. We believe that further research into this form of teacher-student interaction will reveal not only more about the self-management of language learning, but also about the ways in which it can be enhanced through talk. ■

Table 2 Framework for Advisory Sessions

Dialogue agenda	Monitoring (by advisor)	Learner outcomes
Unfold the problem	learner's acknowledgement of elements of problem	expanded representation of problem
Establish goals	learner's statement of goals	commitment to more specific goals
Explore beliefs	learner's engagement in (explicit) discussion of beliefs	heightened awareness of own beliefs

Notes

1   'Task' in this article is used to refer generally to a problematic activity – in this case not a pedagogical task but the higher level task of learning a language.
2   This assumes that language learning is comparable to other types of problem solving.
3   All names in this paper are pseudonyms.

References

Dörnyei, Z. (1998) Motivation in second and foreign language learning. *Language Teaching*, 31:117-35.

Flavell, J.H. (1979) Metacognition and cognitive monitoring: A new area of cognitive developmental inquiry. *American Psychologist*, 34,10:906-11.

Locke, E. A. and Latham, G. P. (1990) *A Theory of Goal Setting and Task Performance*. Englewood Cliffs, NJ.: Prentice Hall.

Newell, A. and Simon, H. A. (1972) *Human Problem Solving*. Englewood Cliffs, NJ.: Prentice-Hall.

Skehan, P. (1998) *A Cognitive Approach to Language Learning*. Oxford: Oxford University Press.

Stern, H. H. (1990) Analysis and experience as variables in second language pedagogy. In B. Harley, P. Allen, J. Cummins, and M. Swain (eds) *The Development of Second Language Proficiency*. Cambridge: Cambridge University Press.

Wenden, A. (1998) Metacognitive knowledge and language learning. *Applied Linguistics*, 19,4:515-37.

◆ Approaches to advising for self-directed language learning

◆ Approches du tutorat en apprentissage des langues auto-guidé

Richard Pemberton, Sarah Toogood,
Susanna Ho and Jacqueline Lam
Hong Kong University of Science and Technology

Abstract

This paper describes the approaches of four advisers involved in a self-directed language-learning programme for postgraduate learners. The programme is the subject of a two-year action research project and has just finished its second year of implementation. Drawing on data from tape-recorded interviews and advising sessions, we report on the approaches of the advisers towards advising and the learners' perceptions of the role of adviser. Finally, we discuss the benefits of this kind of research for the development of advising skills.

Résumé

Cet article décrit les approches de quatre conseillers impliqués dans un programme d'apprentissage linguistique auto-dirigé destiné à des étudiants en troisième cycle d'études universitaires. Ce programme est l'objet d'un projet de recherche sur deux ans et vient d'achever sa deuxième année de mise en place. En utilisant des données issues d'entretiens et de séances de conseil enregistrées, les auteurs rapportent les approches des conseillers et les représentations de l'apprenant de leur rôle. Enfin, ils discutent des avantages de ce genre de recherche pour le développement des stratégies chez le conseiller.

Introduction

Recently there has been increasing interest in the ways that teachers can and do 'advise' or 'counsel' learners when supporting their self-directed language learning (e.g. Gremmo, 1995; Kelly, 1996; Riley, 1997; Voller et al., 1997; Carter, this volume). One of the main research focuses in this area is likely to be the discourse of advising. This has been recently highlighted as an important and fruitful area of future research (Gremmo and Riley, 1995; Riley, 1997), after pioneering work over many years at the Centre de Recherches et d'Applications Pédagogiques en Langues (CRAPEL) at Université Nancy 2 (e.g. Régent, 1993, cited in Riley, 1997; Gremmo, 1995). This paper looks at the language of advising within a university setting in Hong Kong.

At Hong Kong University of Science and Technology (HKUST), we run a self-directed language-learning programme for postgraduate students. The programme is the subject of a two-year Action Learning project, whose aim is to evaluate and enhance the effectiveness of adviser support for self-directed language learning in the programme. In this paper, we briefly report on what we have learned so far of the approaches towards advising of the advisers involved in the programme. We also report how the advisers have changed their approaches in the second year of the programme. We hope to illustrate the benefits of action research when implementing innovative programmes of this type.

The programme The Postgraduate Self-Access English Programme is described in detail in Pemberton et al. (1999). It is an optional one-semester course, carrying no credit. Learners are introduced to the concepts and practice of self-directed learning through eight hours of introductory workshops. After this, they are expected to carry out approximately 30 hours of self-directed language learning over a ten-week period. Each learner has an adviser who supports their learning. Course requirements are that learners should meet their adviser for a total of three hours during the semester, and that they should submit a learning portfolio at the end of semester, containing learning plans and diaries, samples of learning carried out, and an evaluative report. The aims of the programme are twofold: to help participants develop their language skills in a particular area, and to help them develop their ability to direct their own learning.

The learners and the advisers So far, approximately 50 students have opted to take the course each year. The majority of these have been from mainland China, with the second largest group being from Hong Kong. English levels have ranged from Lower Intermediate to Advanced. Each year we chose four learners as a focus for our investigation into the advising that we provided. All agreed to participate in the data collection, which included the audio-recording of three advising sessions and two interviews with a Research Assistant. All advising sessions and interviews were conducted in English.

The advisers are all experienced language learners and teachers of English at tertiary level in Hong Kong. All belong to the Self-Access Centre (SAC) team at HKUST (three having had many years' involvement) and have had previous experience of running self-directed language-learning projects. At the time of starting the programme, we had not undergone any training in advising, but, through our experience as advisers in the SAC, and through our weekly sharing of ideas, assumed that we had similar approaches.

The four advisers involved in the project are referred to (in random order) as A1, A2, A3 and A4. All advisers are referred to as 'she'.

Data collection tools Data was collected each year from the following sources:

- pre- and post-programme questionnaires given to all learners
- tape-recordings of at least three advising sessions for each of the four selected learners
- two tape-recorded interviews with each of the selected learners about their expectations and perceptions of the different advising sessions (conducted by our Research Assistant)
- tape-recorded interviews with advisers about their expectations of and approach to advising (conducted by David Gardner of Hong Kong University)
- a tape-recorded discussion about advising involving the four advisers
- learners' and advisers' diaries
- end-of-programme reports written by the learners and advisers
- e-mail communication between learners and advisers

Adviser approaches

Findings from the first year The most noticeable feature in the transcripts was that the advisers differed in the directiveness of their advice. Three of the advisers (those with greater previous experience of advising) played down their suggestions with expressions of doubt For example, A3 made plentiful use of 'may' and 'maybe', often put suggestions in the form of questions (e.g. 'So why don't you choose one piece of news a day?'; 'Do you think it's useful to compare with someone in the class who you think is good at taking notes?') and presented suggestions as possibilities for consideration:

> After listening to you for some time, do you want to hear some of my advice? [L3: OK.] But I'm not sure if it is useful or not because everyone is different so we will have to try and see which method is best for you. (From first advising session)

Similarly, A2 regularly down-played her suggestions:

> Perhaps you should look at different ways of connecting sentences ... I'm not sure if this works but...

> And it might be an idea to just try and focus, perhaps the things that you're working on...

> I don't know if it will work. But you can have a try. (From second advising session)

A1 used similarly tentative language and tended to qualify demands that the programme required her to make on the learner:

So if you can send me, say, by the end of next week, if you can send me a copy of your diary and it can be on paper like that or you can send me e-mail. Doesn't matter. [...] So you'll e-mail me next week. [L1: OK.] OK. Lovely. And I'll have a look at any problems that you've got. [L1: If I have some problem, I can] e-mail me. Yeah. I hope you get a bit of sleep. All right. Bye bye! (From second advising session)[1]

By contrast, A4 frequently couched her suggestions and encouragements in imperatives and modal verbs expressing obligation:

If you want to change your plan, OK. If you want to change your material, OK. If you want to change your time, OK. But remember that when you are learning, you have to practise – don't give up. Remember, practice makes perfect.

But then you have to come to the last point: revision. Never, never forget revision if you want to remember what you have learned ... Always remember ... Don't forget to revise or else you will forget what you are doing.

Try to learn those more frequent words first because they appear all the time.

A4 said that she would 'shift to a directive mode' of advising when learners were having difficulties with their learning or not meeting the requirements of the course, or wanted a 'tell-me-how-to-do-it' approach from the adviser. She felt that this was appreciated by those who were in difficulties[2]:

They said 'You are the adviser. We expect you to tell us something', so I usually start with telling them because they didn't have many ideas. ... For the student who did not know what he or she was doing, then I would become very directive. And in that way I felt that they were happy, I mean happier than if I just leave them in the dark and ask them to think or give them a lot of choices.

Another difference between A4 and the other advisers in the first year of the programme is that A4 appeared to focus more openly on the course requirements than the other advisers, although all said that they were (to varying degrees) directive in this regard. A4 made it very clear what was expected of the learners in terms of commitment and 'deliverables'. Here is one example:

You have to remember one thing, one very important thing. One very important thing is that in our course three hours per week is important, three hours per week is important. OK. So this is the basic requirement. [...] You have to really try to make the three hours per week because this is the requirement. The requirement is important, all right? This is very important. (From first advising session)

Findings from the second year At the end of the first year, we discussed the transcripts of the advising sessions and of the interviews with each adviser. We also watched *One to One Consultations*, an adviser development video produced at the University of Hong Kong (Voller, 1998). As a result of our discussions, we decided to be firm about course requirements in the second year while at the same time trying to ensure that we did not control the direction of the learning for the learner. Not surprisingly, the most obvious change in advising styles in the second year was exhibited by A4. On several occasions, when her advisee asked her for advice, she first asked him what he thought. This sometimes resulted in the learner thinking through answers to his own questions, e.g.:

> L4: Do you think it is better to divide the three-hour into two or three separate sections?
> A4: So what do you think first?
> L4: Er ... for me to allocate one three-hour is more practical because I don't need to squeeze out time ... different time from different days. But I find [...] it's quite difficult for you to concentrate at the end of the session.
> A4: That's true.
> L4: So in terms of efficiency, maybe it's better to divide a three-hour session into at least two one-and-half-hour sessions. But then you need to find out suitable time for you ... for me at least.

Then, when giving advice, she tended to present options, as in the dialogue below (continuing the discussion above):

> A4: That is true. Actually I mean, basically people usually believe that language needs practice, right? The more you practise, the better you are, you would be. [...] (explains why) So in my opinion, I also think that it's better to split, I mean use different times slots in a week to study. However, since you have a very tight schedule [...] then you put it in one slot with three hours which is what you have said. [...] What you can do is that maybe in the first one and a half hours, you can study one type of material, and then take a break, five-minute break, and then change to another type of materials. [...] In this case, you can focus either on accuracy in the first hour or fluency [...] so in this case, you make the three hours easier. What do you think? But myself, I have my opinion. I would feel to split it in different days is better [...] will be more beneficial for yourself.
> L4: I think I have to look back to my timetable first. So if I can find two one-and-half hour free time for me within my timetable, so I will ... my first priority is to ... to use two one-and-half hour session.
> A4: Good.
> L4: Then if ... but if I can't find this ... if I find this option is not possible, then I will stick to one three-hour session.
> A4: Then after that maybe you decide what to do with that three hours.
> L4: Yes.

As her advisee confirmed, 'She used to give a list of options from expertise and then the final decision is upon me.' The second year transcripts showed that A4 also expressed her suggestions much more tentatively than before. Compared with her advising style in the first year of the programme, this represented a major change.

But while A4 became markedly less directive in her advising, two other advisers surprisingly appeared to become more directive. A3 occasionally set short-term goals for her advisee:

> A3: Next time when you come and see me, could you promise me … well, I think maybe I can give you a little pressure. I don't know if you like it or not because … let me know if you don't like it.
>
> L3: No problem. Up to …
>
> A3: So what I suggest is maybe next time when you come to me again, you could finish a certain number of chapters or even half of the book. So that's your goal during Easter.
>
> L3: Yeah. Yeah. That's a good idea.

On one occasion, A2 also jumped in to give directive advice on the content of the learner's plan:

> L2: I also find in my recording, I can't … I'm not clear which area I should use the emphasis … I should leave the stress.
>
> A2: Right. I think what we can do is we can change your focus now. We don't have much more time on the programme.

As in the example above, there was much use of the word 'we' in A2's first advising session with this learner, suggesting that the adviser was helper and collaborator, but also taking some of the responsibility for planning away from the learner. A2 was also occasionally directive when it came to advising about learning methods:

> One piece of advice if you want to do that, though, would be that you should actually write out what you want to say in the presentation … word by word. […] If you're working on the pronunciation, it's quite important to have the words in front of you.

In the above example, A2 is suggesting one of her favourite methods, a technique that worked very well for her as a learner. In her enthusiasm for the method, she appears to attempt to make a decision for the learner.

To varying degrees, we've seen all the advisers exhibit tendencies to intervene in the learning process (whether consciously or unconsciously) and feel it necessary for advisers to be aware of the danger that learners' ability to develop their self-directed learning might be undermined, if these tendencies are not guarded against.

Advising strategies

Overall, our advising sessions appear to involve the features and communication strategies listed by Voller (1998). He identifies key features of the first consultation (goal setting, narrowing down goals etc.) and what he calls the 'Feedback loop' (identifying problems, evaluating progress, advising, teaching etc.), and the communication strategies of Active Listening (restating, eliciting etc.) and Motivating (empathising, encouraging etc.). Our analysis of our advising strategies is not yet complete, but a preliminary listing is below:

Asking questions
　　Eliciting (information, goals, progress, beliefs, feelings etc.)
　　Probing
　　Passing the learner's question back to them

Clarifying
　　Requesting clarification
　　Restating
　　Summarising
　　Interpreting
　　Checking comprehension
　　Highlighting contradictions in what the learner has said/planned

Advising
　　Helping analyse needs
　　Helping focus goals
　　Identifying possible problems in the learner's plan/learning method
　　Reminding the learner of their original goals/plan
　　Offering suggestions re: planning; record-keeping (writing of plan, diaries, portfolio report); time allocation; materials and activities; (alternative) learning strategies; evaluation
　　Providing feedback
　　Evaluating progress and/or performance
　　Providing information on language features and/or terminology (e.g. accents, contraction etc.)

Motivating
　　Encouraging/praising
　　Empathising
　　Mentioning experiences of other learners (including the adviser)
　　Agreeing

Our listing has elements in common with Voller's (1998) key consultation features and strategies, Kelly's (1996) macro- and micro-skills for language counselling, and Régent's (1993; cited in Riley, 1997) counselling roles. There is also overlap between the four main functional areas (e.g. questions are asked in order to clarify; advice or evaluation given may motivate the learner) and there is no indication yet of the frequency or importance of the different strategies. However, we think the list will be useful in focusing our attention and that of our colleagues, on four major features of advising discourse.

Learner views of the role of advisor
The changes in A4's approach to advising in the second year reflect the

changes that have taken place in all of us as we've learned (and continue to learn) to control the impulse to teach. This change seems to have been picked up on by the learners. When asked to characterise the approach of their adviser (from a choice of 'Just listened'; 'Listened and suggested several options'; 'Listened and told me what to do'; 'Just told me what to do') they chose 'Listened and suggested several options'. They also said they liked this style:

> I think it's up to me to choose some method, but her provision of some options is very important.

As in the first year, the great majority said that the advising helped them to learn independently, and that after the programme they feel able to carry out their learning without an appointed adviser. As one student put it:

> The advising helps me to know the right way to solve the problem and I solve it by myself actually.

It is interesting to note, as the above comment nicely illustrates, many of our learners seem to see the ability to learn independently as being facilitated by some sort of problem-solving on the part of the adviser. The adviser is seen as an 'expert' whose expertise is to be tapped in a way which relates to the learner's needs, and as a motivational element in the learning process.

Of the four selected advisees in the second year, three mentioned that their adviser gave suggestions to help them solve their problems (Adviser as Problem-Solving Aid); two mentioned that their advisers provided pressure or force (Adviser as Pressuriser); one that their adviser helped them stay on track to achieve their learning goals (Adviser as Guide); and one that their adviser provided encouragement (Adviser as Companion/Support).

That many students are using us as Problem-solving Aids is not necessarily a bad thing – what counts is who identifies and solves the problems. And it is certainly a step forward from using us as Tutors. We will not go into the issue of cultural and institutional influences on our learners here (see Pemberton & Toogood, forthcoming). But student responses suggest that, in our particular situation, our approach to advising for self-directed language learning is not too wide of the mark.[3]

Conclusion

The evidence from the advising session transcripts of A1, A2 and A3 in the second year of the programme show that trying to support autonomy within the framework of established course requirements is not easy. We feel that an adviser's approach is affected by a number of factors which influence levels of directiveness:

- length of time given for advising sessions
- the difficulty in separating (or blending?) the need to ensure that students meet course requirements with the role of giving advice in support of self-directed learning
- our students' perception of the adviser as someone to motivate and

encourage but also as someone who is an expert in the field
- the fact that advisers are trained as teachers
- the need to justify the effectiveness of autonomous learning to the authorities, other colleagues, and the students themselves

Investigating our advising has been an eye-opening process and we have developed a great deal as a result of it – both individually and as a team. Amongst other things, we have learned the importance of:

- not assuming that we share the same beliefs
- guarding against the temptation to recommend our own favourite learning methods (assuming that problems will fit ready-made solutions)
- conducting ongoing research in order to inform our advising practice

It is our belief that this kind of research is a powerful learning tool. Some of the factors contributing to its success in this case seem to be:

- its combination of action and reflection
- its use of data from a variety of sources, including interviews to probe/clarify matters that were unclear in earlier data
- regular meetings
- a small, committed team

Apart from the work at CRAPEL, little research has been published so far on the discourse of advising. We see it as vital that advisers like ourselves start to analyse how we advise, and develop training materials or activities based on that analysis (cf. Bailly, 1995; Voller, 1998).[4] The very process of self-analysis is, as Riley (1997:131) says, 'a highly formative one for the individuals concerned'. And the results of this kind of analysis will be of use not only to other advisers but also to teachers interested in promoting self-directed learning in their classrooms. ▨

Acknowledgements

We would like to thank Sye Sui-kam and David Gardner for all their help in the data collection for this project. We also gratefully acknowledge the financial support provided by the Action Learning Project (University Grants Committee of Hong Kong).

Notes

1   It is feasible that A1's use of conditionals and expressions of concern for L1's health gave the opposite force from that intended. L1 appears to have picked up on the conditional form of the request ('If I have some problem, I can [e-mail you]') rather than the direct force intended by A1 ('So you'll e-mail me next week'). The result: no e-mail was received!
2   In this she was undoubtedly correct. However, the advice given by the other advisers, although not directive, was also rated positively by the students.
3   The following comments are representative: 'The flexibility of learning and the advices and helps from the advisor is a good combination.' 'In this course, I was fully in charge of what I would learn and it gave me a opportunity to focus my limited study time on the area what my weakness was […]. The course enabled me to take the initiative to choose when and how to learn. At the same time, my Self-Access Adviser gave me the constant support and guided and advised me as I carried my self-access learning. After this course, I not only improved my English, especially in pronunciation, but also knowed how to learn English by Self-Access.
4   An example in this area is the work of Marina Mozzon-McPherson at the University of Hull.

References

Bailly, S. (1995) La formation de conseiller. *Mélanges Pédagogiques*, 22:63–83.

Crabbe, D., Hoffmann, A. and Cotterall, S. Examining the Discourse of Learner Advisory Sessions. *AILA Review* (this volume).

Gremmo, M-J. (1995) Conseiller n'est pas enseigner: le rôle du conseiller dans l'entretien de conseil. *Mélanges Pédagogiques*, 22:33–61.

Gremmo, M-J. and Riley, P. (1995) Autonomy, self-direction and self-access in language teaching and learning: the history of an idea. *System*, 23,2:151-64.

Kelly, R. (1996) Language counselling for learner autonomy: the skilled helper in self-access learning. In R. Pemberton, E.S.L. Li, W.W. F. Or and H.D. Pierson (eds) *Taking Control: autonomy in language learning.* Hong Kong University Press.

Mozzon-McPherson, M., and Vismans, R. (eds) (forthcoming) *Beyond Language Teaching towards Language Advising.* London: CILT.

Pemberton, R., Toogood, S., Ho. S., and Lam, J. (forthcoming) Learner and adviser expectations in a self-directed language-learning programme: a case study of four learners and four advisers. In D. Bickerton and M. Gotti (eds) *5th CercleS Conference Proceedings.*

Pemberton, R., Ho, S., Lam, J. and Toogood, S. (1999) Developing a self-directed English language-learning programme for postgraduate students. In B. Morrison (ed.) *Proceedings of the HASALD Conference 2000: helping learners to help themselves – the development of independence from primary to tertiary.* Hong Kong Polytechnic University.

Régent, O. (1993) Communication, strategy and language learning. In J.L. Otal and M.L. Villanueva (eds) *Primeves Jornades sobre Auto-aprenentatge de Llengües.* Castelló: Publicacions de la Universitat Jaume.

Riley, P. (1997) The guru and the conjurer: aspects of counselling for self-access. In P. Benson and P.Voller (eds) *Autonomy and Independence in Language Learning.* London: Longman.

Voller, P. (1998) *One to One Consultations.* (Video and guidebook) English Centre: University of Hong Kong.

Voller, P., Martyn, E. and Pickard, V. (1997) Helping learners help themselves: counselling for autonomy in a self-access centre. In D. Kember, B.H. Lam, L.Yan, J.C.K.Yum and S.B. Liu (eds) *Case Studies of Improving Teaching and Learning from the Action Learning Project.* Action Learning Project: Hong Kong Polytechnic University.

◆ # From awareness to counselling in learner autonomy

◆ # De la conscience au conseil en autonomie de l'apprenant

Beverly Ann Carter
University of the West Indies, Trinidad and Tabago

Abstract

This paper underscores the need for teachers to be aware of the educational background of their learners when promoting autonomy in language learning. It contends that the first phase of an intervention to promote autonomy must be an investigation of the learners' previous educational background in order to gauge its influence on their willingness to assume responsibility for their learning. Drawing on data from the autobiographies of a group of advanced foreign-language learners which show that the learners have traditionally relied very heavily on their teachers as managers of their learning, this paper discusses the implications of such findings. The paper contends that autonomy can be fostered by engaging the learners in a counselling programme using a context-sensitive model to meet the needs identified in the analysis of their autobiographies.

Resume

Cet article met en relief la nécessité pour les enseignants d'avoir conscience de l'histoire éducative de leurs apprenants lorsqu'ils veulent accroître la part de l'autonomie dans l'apprentissage d'une langue. Il y est établi que la première phase d'une action de développement de l'autonomie doit consister en une investigation de l'arrière-plan éducatif des apprenants visant à établir jusqu'à quel point ils ont envie de gérer leurs propres apprentissages. Se basant sur des données autobiographiques d'un groupe d'apprenants avancés qui montrent que ceux-ci se sont fortement reposés sur leurs professeurs comme gestionnaires de leurs apprentissages, l'article discute des implications d'une telle situation. Il soutient l'idée que l'autonomie peut être développée si on engage les apprenants dans un programme de soutien/conseil réglé en fonction des besoins identifiés par l'analyse des autobiographies.

Background to the study

One factor that determines students' readiness to benefit from an autonomous approach to learning is their previous educational experiences. While it is generally accepted that the promotion of autonomy in any context is likely to require a considerable attitudinal change for learners, a shift to autonomy poses an even greater challenge for teacher-dependent students. How much of an attitudinal change is required is difficult for teachers to ascertain, unless concrete steps are taken to investigate the learners' previous educational experiences.

In Trinidad and Tobago, the context where this study was conducted, there is a growing concern among educators (Ministry of Education, 1994) about the effects of a highly competitive examination system on students' learning. Researchers in other contexts (cf. Pierson, 1998) have posited a causal link between public examinations and students' learning. Paris (1998), in his critique of achievement testing in the United States, makes claims about the distortion of student behaviours in the face of what he labels 'high stakes testing'. Yet, in spite of this research which points to a link between educational context and poor learning behaviours, it is generally assumed that university entrants have somehow mastered the skills of learning by virtue of their successful passage through primary and secondary education.

This paper reports on an attempt to address the lack of knowledge about a group of learners' educational background as it relates to their foreign language learning. It contends that any intervention to promote learner autonomy must be informed by an investigation into the educational background of the learners and its influence on their foreign language learning. It suggests that only when teachers are fully aware of their learners' background will they be able to provide support in the form of a counselling programme to retrain learners in learning how to learn.

The learners' educational background

A brief review of the significant milestones at primary and secondary level for the average university entrant in French will allow for a better understanding of his/her educational background. The undergraduate learner of French has sat highly competitive public examinations at ages 11-plus, 16-plus, and 18-plus. In the 11-plus examination, the student of French would most likely have placed among the top quartile of candidates and been assigned to one of the traditional grammar schools, since the teaching of French is largely confined to these schools. At 16-plus, this student would have been once again part of a select group (roughly 20% of the total secondary school population) to have earned a place in the Advanced level programme. Finally, to satisfy matriculation requirements of the University of the West Indies, the 18-plus student must attain a passing grade at the Advanced level in at least two subjects and a General Paper.

Public examinations, stressing summative assessment, are thus an important feature of the educational landscape in this context. Their importance is judged to be critical by most students and their parents, and as a result students often seek extra coaching, in addition to their regular classroom tuition, to prepare for their examinations. As a result of the highly competitive nature of the education system, students come to rely heavily on the guidance of experts – the subject teacher and private tutor – to steer them to success. One consequence of this is that despite attempts by many classroom teachers, particularly at the secondary level, to encourage more student-centred approaches, students and their parents often prefer didactic, teacher-directed learning, which they feel is more likely to guarantee examination success.

In contrast to the teacher-directed learning in which students engage at the primary and secondary level, students who continue on to higher education, having 'learned only the skills of being taught' (Knowles, 1988) are ill-equipped to engage in the kind of self-directed learning expected of them at this level. Their lecturers, on the other hand, are seldom fully aware of the constraints posed by the students' previous learning, knowing only that the students' passivity and lack of initiative are detrimental to their success in higher education.

In promoting learner autonomy among undergraduates who were advanced learners of French, it became clear that to shift learners from the kind of learning to which they had become accustomed to self-directed learning would require an important attitudinal change. First, however, the teacher-researcher would need to investigate the learners' educational background to determine how the learners' present attitudes had been formed by their previous educational experiences. Then, armed with a better awareness of the kinds of attitudes and skills that students brought to their learning, a teacher or language advisor could implement a counselling programme to help learners learn how to learn.

The study

Twenty-eight undergraduates, approximately 80% of those enrolled in the first year French language course in the 1997-98 academic year, submitted learner autobiographies, 'their personal L2 learning history' (Matsumoto, 1994: p. 367) as part of their learner autonomy project. This reflective writing which was to be done at home and submitted one week after the start of the learner autonomy project, would enable both the learners themselves and their teachers to become aware of the most influential factors in their language learning history. Learners were therefore requested to use their auto-biographical account, which was the initial entry of their diaries or journals[1], to reflect on their first exposure to foreign languages, their school experiences in foreign language learning and their previous language teachers. Learners wrote in English or in the target language, providing candid insights into the factors surrounding their initial and continuing foreign language learning.

Results and discussion

The autobiographies revealed that 75% of the learners had begun their formal language learning in a school setting, while the remaining 25% noted that their first exposure to foreign languages had come in a naturalistic setting, either at home or during travel. All but two students reported that their first foreign language exposure had been a positive one. Those learners who had first heard a foreign language spoken by family members remembered their fascination and delight on hearing a strange language. Classroom learners had equally vivid memories of their first foreign language exposure, often comparing the experience to falling in love:

- I instantly fell in love with the French language.
- *Pour moi c'était l'amour à première vue.* (For me it was love at first sight.)
- It was then and there that I experienced a passion for this romantic language.

Classroom learners gave credit to their teachers, whom they described as 'wonderful', 'fascinating', 'charismatic', 'kind' and 'nice' for sparking their initial interest in the target language. One student summarised her appreciation of her teachers in the following way, '*Je pense que les profs étaient un facteur-clé pourquoi j'adore les langues. Mon prof de français, Mr. C., était excellent à mon avis.*' ('I think that the teachers were really the most important reason why I grew to love foreign languages. I think that my French teacher, Mr. C., was excellent'). The strong bond that developed between the learners and their language teachers was a factor which emerged repeatedly in the data.

The second related theme that emerged in the content analysis of the diaries was the learners' perceptions of the characteristics of a good or bad teacher. Whereas 'bad' teachers inspired fear, or were incompetent, 'good' teachers demonstrated a wide range of behaviours. Among the qualities that learners valued positively were their teachers' ability to motivate, to be creative, to inspire, to express empathy for their students and above all show their professional competence. The teachers' mastery of the target language and their competence at guiding their charges through the syllabus in fifth and sixth Form (the years of the all-important Public Exams) emerged as salient factors in the students' foreign language classroom experience:

- I had the same French teacher for five years. She was very thorough. She prepared us well for (the) CXC (examination).
- I must say that my old school had a very good language department. The teachers were very good.
- Spanish was good. The teacher was competent and thorough.

The repeated emphasis on teacher performance – about 45% of the students mentioned their teachers' competence or lack of competence in their autobiographies – closely links to another factor which emerged as significant in the data. There was a clear trend among students to see teaching and learning as two contiguous activities. Many learners failed to distinguish between teaching and learning as related but separate activities. Learners tended to equate good teaching with successful learning and blame unsuccessful learning on poor teaching. The student who stated '*Les professeurs n'étaient pas les bons enseignants et j'ai appris très peu.*' ('The teachers were not very good at their jobs and I learned very little.') perhaps best exemplifies that attitude.

Only two students out of the 28 in the study, wrote about achieving success in their foreign language learning in spite of the teacher. One learner's determination to succeed in the face of a number of unfortunate circumstances, '*j'étais déterminée de ne perdre pas ma passion pour les langues … rien n'a changé.*' ('I was determined not to lose my zeal for foreign languages … nothing had changed.') is in sharp contrast to the majority of her peers. Another student who was a graduate of the same school adopted an attitude that was diametrically opposite to her peer's, blaming her inexperienced teacher and the school administration for her poor performance in French, '*Ici, nous préparions pour un examen majeur et il nous donne un prof sans l'expérience d'apprendre à l'école ou même avec la façon de CXC.*' ('Here we were, preparing for a major exam and they give us someone with no previous teaching experience and who furthermore knew nothing of the syllabus demands for the CXC examination.'). This student was emphatic that there was a direct causal link between the change of teacher and her loss of confidence and subsequent poor performance in French.

Among those students who did not directly address the issue of teacher competence in their autobiographies, there was nevertheless, implicit in their comments the notion that their success in language learning was linked to their good fortune to have had the same teacher for a long period of time: in the words of one student, '*J'avais de la chance car j'ai gardé le même professeur de français jusqu'en terminale.*' ('I was lucky to have kept the same French teacher straight through to upper sixth form').

Another factor identified as important to learning in two accounts was the attitude of other students in the class. Peer behaviour was identified by those students as a negative influence. One student wrote 'It wasn't an atmosphere that was conducive to work', while the second student who expressed a negative evaluation of her peers said 'The class was not what I expected, every attempt I made to improve my language was met with resistance from other class members'. There were no instances of students reporting a positive, cooperative classroom atmosphere in which they saw their peers as partners in language learning. Little mention was made of group or project work in or out of class as significant events in the students' foreign language learning. There were only two students who recalled group activities: one referred to her membership in the French and Spanish clubs at her school as a positive, enriching experience; the other recalled the many activities in which her class engaged, from plays and French competitions, to hosting a French Day at her school.

In summing up, although to the researcher it seems unlikely that only one student had a rich variety of experiences in her foreign language learning, what is important here is how learners conceptualised their past learning in French. For 45% of students – a significant number – learning the target language was conceptualised in terms of the teaching act: good teaching leading to good learning or bad teaching leading to bad learning. Additionally among this sub-group, three diarists wrote of their recourse or lack of recourse to out-of-school tutoring to remedy the perceived deficiencies of their classroom teacher. Two students recalled their personal, solitary struggle to overcome the difficulties they were experiencing in class. Learning in the minds of many students seemed to be something that was done or not done to them. There is no indication in the data that students accepted ownership of their own learning. When the teacher as agent of learning failed to perform satisfactorily, learners felt compelled to seek help in the form of other tutors, bemoan their fate, or in two cases reluctantly assume responsibility for their own learning.

The analysis of the learners' autobiographical data provided a further insight into the factors pertaining to their foreign language learning. Although the question of mastery of the four skills and grammar was a frequent theme in subsequent diary entries submitted by the students, in their learner autobiographies only 10 of the students, about 35% of the group, explored aspects of their foreign language proficiency. These learners focused on their strengths and weaknesses in language learning and their preference for the different modalities: speaking as opposed to writing or reading as opposed to listening. Six learners expressed their uncertainty about having strong enough grammar mastery for further study, while the remaining four felt that listening was the most challenging skill.

The contrast between the predominant focus on skill mastery in subsequent entries and the relatively peripheral role they played in the autobiographies underscores how the autobiographies served a different function from the main diary-keeping assignment. Whereas the students used their journals to record their daily difficulties and challenges with the language, the autobiographical accounts focused on the major themes, the 'big picture', so to speak, of their language learning. The autobiographies presented the framework of their language learning with highlights of the significant events in their language career. Although the students were not specifically instructed to present a rationale for the kind of language learners they were, this is the information that the autobiography task elicited.

If we were to use this perspective to interpret the data supplied, then the frequent references to the role played by their teachers in their learning assume a far greater importance than the 45% suggests. The assumption by their teachers that undergraduates feel confident to self-direct their learning and the assumption that by virtue of their success at three highly competitive public examinations these students have learnt how to learn, seem to be contradicted by the data which suggest that almost half of the students conceive of learning in terms of whether their teachers have been good or bad managers of their learning: '*Les professeurs n'étaient pas les bons enseignants et j'ai appris très peu*'.

A teacher who wishes to promote autonomy among these or other students from similar backgrounds would be handicapped in his/her efforts to foster autonomy without the kind of knowledge that the autobiographies revealed. It is important, too, that the teacher be aware of the factors underpinning students' attitudes and beliefs early in the course, or valuable time could be lost in implementing an appropriate intervention to promote autonomy. In summary, the autobiographies serve as a sort of needs analysis helping the teacher to determine what measures should be put in place to foster autonomy among learners.

Counselling for learner autonomy

In many contexts where an autonomous approach to language learning is practised, a counsellor or language learning advisor is the person charged with giving learners 'both general and specific advice on language learning'. Moreover, that person helps learners to identify their needs, strengths and weaknesses and helps learners to develop and monitor their individual self-study plans (University of Hull Language Institute Brochure, 1998). In the context where this study was conducted no such provision as yet exists for guiding learners along the route to autonomy. Yet there is a clear need for a counselling approach to meet the needs of the learners that have been identified in their autobiographies. If learners were to persist in seeing their learning as dependent on classroom teaching or private tuition, their ability to maximise the opportunities for learning that exist in the foreign language programme at the University of the West Indies, St. Augustine, would be severely constrained. The first focus of a counselling approach therefore must be to bring students to the realisation that 'each participant, teacher and learner, has a distinct responsibility for achievement. Good teaching is not enough for high achievement. Good learning, the active mental contribution of the learner, is a necessary component' (Wittrock, 1986: p. 306).

Counselling for learner autonomy in our context must involve the teacher in adopting some of the roles that are now held by advisors and counsellors in self-access or open access centres. In the absence of a full-time counsellor, innovative approaches must be tried to ensure that the teacher is not overburdened by the additional responsibilities, and can encourage learners to participate actively in seeking solutions to their problems. One way in which this could be done is by adopting a collaborative approach, drawing on a model which is familiar to the learners in this context: the model of the 'gayap' which is a community-based collaborative project.

In a gayap, members of a community come together to achieve some clearly defined task. There are clear guidelines in a gayap and these can be used to structure the counselling interaction. The initial stage in the process is needs identification: an individual identifies a task which must be accomplished. That person then addresses him/herself to members of the community with an appeal for help and in the understanding that all members are free to contribute according to the skills which they possess. For the learner who is in the process of acquiring autonomy, the collaborative project of the gayap would imply that:

1   s/he identifies needs
2   s/he appeals to all the human resources available – teachers and peers
3   in collaboration with his/her learning partners the process and product
    of the task are clearly defined

Since the learner is familiar with the concept of the gayap s/he can easily understand the important parameters of the process – needs identification, collaboration, active participation in the task by the beneficiary. The flexible framework of the gayap nonetheless allows for some modification to be made as the situation demands and this might become necessary in adopting the model in a counselling approach. One modification might be to the part played by the teacher in his/her role of counsellor. The teacher, in assuming a counsellor role, might need to help learners to identify their needs in the initial stages. Counselling might therefore need to be done in two modes in the traditional one-to-one interaction, where the teacher counsels the individual student, and in the collaborative gayap mode where other learners participate in the counselling process. But in the initial phases of the counselling process, it is the teacher who must draw on the awareness gained from analysing the learners' autobiographies to give the learners general and specific advice about the competencies necessary to be successful managers of their own learning.

Conclusion
This study has posited that teachers who wish to foster an autonomous approach need to be aware of the attitudes and beliefs which advanced foreign language learners bring to their language learning. It suggests that a failure to investigate the rationale for learners' behaviour could prove inimical to the promotion of autonomy. The next step – the counselling of the learners – must be flexible and context-sensitive to meet the particular needs of the learners for whom it is intended. ▨

Note
1   No distinction is made between journals and diaries in this paper.

References
Knowles, M. (1988) Preface. In D. Boud (ed.) *Developing Student Autonomy in Learning.* London: Kogan Page.

Matsumoto, K. (1994) Introspection, verbal reports and second language learning strategy research. *The Canadian Modern Language Review,* 50:363-86.

Ministry of Education. (1994) *Policy paper 1993-2000.* National Task Force on Education White Paper. Port of Spain, Trinidad and Tobago: Ministry of Education.

Paris, S.G. (1998) Why learner-centered assessment is better than high-stakes testing. In N. Lambert and B. McCombs (eds) *How Students Learn. Reforming schools through learner-centered education.* Washington D.C. : American Psychological Association.

Pierson, H. (1996) Learner culture and learner autonomy in the Hong Kong Chinese context. In Pemberton, Li et al. (eds) *Taking Control: autonomy in language learning.* Hong Kong: Hong Kong University Press.

University of Hull. (1998) *Language Institute Brochure.* Hull: University of Hull.

Wittrock, M. C. (1986) Students' thought processes. In M.C. Wittrock (ed.) *Handbook of Research on Teaching.* New York: Macmillan.

◆ Towards an analytic approach to assessing learner autonomy

◆ Vers une approche analytique de l'évaluation de l'autonomie de l'apprenant

Jose Lai

The Chinese University of Hong Kong

Abstract

Learner training or learning to learn as a pedagogical practice has received increased attention over the past decade or so. Although positive outcomes have been reported on learners' increased capacity for self-direction in language learning through learner training, most findings tend to be descriptive rather than empirical. This is probably due to a lack of validated measurement scales for assessing the construct 'self-direction' in language learning. This paper aims to (1) address the urgent need of adopting a more analytical approach to assessing learners' capacity for self-direction, and (2) more importantly, introduce two validated measurement scales developed to assess learners' self-direction, both at the micro (task) and macro (overall organisation) levels of their language learning process. It is believed that these scales will find universal utility in settings in which learner training is implemented. The rationale, development and validation of these measurement scales will form the core of the discussion.

Résumé

En tant que pratique pédagogique, apprendre à gérer son propre apprentissage ou apprendre à apprendre ne cesse, depuis une décennie, d'attirer l'attention des specialistes en ce domaine. Bien que des preuves aient été fournies par de récentes recherches sur la capacité des apprenants à gérer leur propre apprentissage grâce à un entraînement approprié, la plupart de ces études sont de nature plutôt descriptive qu'empirique. Ceci résulte probablement de l'absence d'une mesure valable pour évaluer le bien-fondé de l'autonomie ('self-direction') dans l'apprentissage des langues. Cette étude a pour buts: premièrement de montrer l'urgente nécessité de l'adoption d'une approche plus analytique en vue de mesurer la capacité d'autonomie des apprenants et, deuxièment, de présenter deux types de dispositifs de mesure destinées à évaluer l'autonomie des apprenants, tous deux opérant à deux niveaux, celui des tâches et celui de l'organisation de l'ensemble de leur processus d'apprentissage d'une langue. Nous pensons que ces dispositifs de mesure seront en mesure de fournir des outils universellement applicables pour la mise en oeuvre d'un programme de formation des apprenants. La logique, le développement et la validation de ces dispositifs de mesure seront examinés en détails.

Introduction

To facilitate objective measurement of how learners' capacity for autonomy in language learning has developed over a course term, two rating scales were constructed. As autonomy is operative at two levels – process control at the task or micro level, and self-direction at the overall process or macro level – two different rating scales need to be developed. This paper describes in detail both the development and validation of these two rating scales. In each case, how and why selected items were identified for rating purposes will be explained. To maintain objectivity, several raters were invited to score for all the entries obtained. To minimise rater effect and ensure consistency, raters were invited to a training session. Notes regarding standardised procedures and guidelines for raters' reference were also prepared. To validate each rating scale, different statistical procedures were employed and these will be described and analysed. In the case of the first rating scale to measure process control, inter-rater consistency was analysed by computing the Spearman Rank-Order Coefficients Alpha for both sets of ratings. In the second rating scale to measure self-direction, both internal consistency of items and inter-rater reliability were addressed. Accordingly, the 'Guttman Odd-Even Split Half' analysis and the Spearman Rank-Order Coefficients Alpha were used.

Development of measurement scale for evaluating process control

Theoretically, process control refers to the learner's ability to self-monitor and self-evaluate her learning tasks and/or learning strategies employed for each learning activity. To measure this construct, it has been operationally defined as a learner's ability to set realistic task aims for a chosen piece of material or activity; identify problems; employ relevant strategies to tackle the problems; and conduct self-assessment of the learning experience with an aim to set future challenges. This process control is operative at the micro level of the learning process – specific learner control of her learning on the task level.

Background In a study to enhance process control, learners were guided to keep a listening journal for every program they listened or watched with the following headings in a table form: Activity/Program, Task Aims, Brief Content Summary, Problems, Strategies and Self-Assessment. In each entry, learners were to select for themselves an activity or program of interest to them, set related task aims for the listening activity, report its brief content, identify the problems confronted in the course of listening, employ or develop relevant strategies to cope with the problems, and conduct a self-assessment of the entire listening activity. Learners were expected to provide three such entries per fortnight. Consequently, a total of 15 entries were collected from each learner throughout the entire course term. However, only the first and last three entries were identified for pre- and post-analysis respectively.

Identification of items for rating To evaluate the extent to which learners increased their control of their learning process (at the task level), only two headings (i.e. Task Aims and Self-Assessment) were identified for analysis. In concrete terms, a four-item, five-point rating scale was used to evaluate all task aims set by individual learners for each programme or activity chosen by themselves, and the self-assessment they conducted after completing the activity.

Three other headings – Content Summary; Problems, and Strategies – were excluded from the evaluations for specific reasons. Since comprehension ability was not a concern at this point, the input on content summary did not appear to warrant attention. Problems and strategies were excluded purely for practical reasons: the input on these two aspects is a function of uncontrollable variables – such as the difficulty level and individual learner's competence in understanding, and their topical knowledge of the selected program – which differ from individual to individual, and from situation to situation. An absence of discussion in these two areas in a learner's work cannot be taken as the fact that learner's inability to discuss them. Indeed, the reverse could be the case. They might be simply too competent for the task at hand and find it too easy and unnecessary to discuss. To include these aspects for the present evaluation purposes would only confound the findings.

The scale and scoring details The scale for evaluating process control comprised four items (two on task aims and two on self-assessment), each of which was to be evaluated by a five-point rating scale. For the task aim(s), there were two criteria for judgement:

1   whether the task aim(s) is/are relevant to the type of
      programme chosen, e.g. to set an aim of 'entertainment' or
      'getting used to informal conversational exchanges' for
      watching a 'comedy' is more relevant than for watching
      a 'news report';
2   whether the aim(s) are conducive to training aspects of
      listening skills/strategies.

For self-assessment, there were also two criteria for judgement:

1   whether the self-assessment conducted is related to the set aim(s);

2   whether the self-assessment conducted is related to the learner's listening process and/or performance.

To construct a rating scale, these criteria were translated into four statements for scoring purposes. The statements for evaluating task aim(s) are as follows:

a   The task aim(s) is/are realistically set for the type of programme chosen;
b   The aim(s) are directly related to specific aspects of listening skills or strategies.

The statements for evaluating self-assessment are as follows:

c   The self-assessment directly addresses the set aims(s);
d   The self-assessment specifically addresses the learner's learning process or performance.

A five-point rating scale (0 to 4) was constructed to determine the degree to which each statement reflected each learning activity recorded. On this rating scale, 1 to 4 represents various degree of relevance: 1 denotes the lowest end of the scale, and 4 denotes the highest. 0 refers to cases of nil answers or descriptions which are not an aim, or totally irrelevant input.

To obtain a more reliable scoring, a total of six entries of activities were assessed for each learner, three at the beginning and three at the end of the course. Students were expected to hand in their listening journals with three separate entries completed over a fortnight. As it would be more reliable to survey a learner's input over a range of activities within a given period, all three activities were assessed to minimise the effect of chance. A mean score was then obtained for analysis.

Validation of the process control measurement scale To determine the reliability of a given scale, the normal practice is to examine its internal consistency among all items included and proceed from there. However, this was found inappropriate with the present scale which comprised only four items (statements a, b, c, d), each of which aimed to examine a rather distinct aspect of the construct under study. A more appropriate alternative was to examine the inter-rater consistency between their scores.

Inter-rater reliability In this connection, two raters were invited to score independently all 99 entries obtained for calculation. To minimise personal bias in judgement, raters were invited for a training session with raters' notes provided for scoring procedures.

Computing correlation coefficients To find the correlation between the two sets of ratings, the Spearman Rank-Order Coefficients Alpha analysis was identified for use. This was preferred since there was no evidence showing that there was a normal distribution of scores at that stage, an assumption to be observed when using other models such as the Cronbach Alpha.

In this statistical exercise, correlation coefficients were calculated rather than reliability coefficients mainly because what was being looked at was how consistent the two raters had been in their scoring. The higher the correlation coefficients, the more reliable was the whole scale and scoring.

Statistical procedures for calculating correlation coefficients

Step 1 Raw scores were computed to calculate descriptives separately for each rater as shown in Tables 1 to 4.

Table 1 Statistics for rater 1 on pre-total scores (pretot1)	
Mean	5.116
Median	4.333
Std Dev	2.694
Variance	7.258
Kurtosis	-0.964
S E Kurt	0.798
Skewness	0.365
S E Skew	0.409
Minimum	1.000
Maximum	10.333
Valid cases	33
Missing cases	38*

Table 2 Statistics for rater 2 on pre-total scores (pretot2)	
Mean	5.823
Median	5.083
Std Dev	2.936
Variance	8.618
Kurtosis	-0.155
S E Kurt	0.809
Skewness	0.648
S E Skew	0.414
Minimum	1.500
Maximum	12.667
Valid cases	32
Missing cases	39*

Table 3 Statistics for rater 1 on post-total scores (postot1)	
Mean	9.010
Median	9.000
Std Dev	3.297
Variance	10.868
Kurtosis	-0.636
S E Kurt	0.582
Skewness	-0.132
S E Skew	0.295
Minimum	1.667
Maximum	15.667
Valid cases	66†
Missing cases	5

Table 4 Statistics for rater 2 on post-total scores (postot2)	
Mean	8.896
Median	8.500
Std Dev	2.962
Variance	8.774
Kurtosis	-0.505
S E Kurt	0.582
Skewness	0.206
S E Skew	0.295
Minimum	3.000
Maximum	15.667
Valid cases	66†
Missing cases	5

* Missing cases mainly refer to one group of learners who were exempt from the initial input for experimental purpose

† Valid cases became double the size in post-test scores because input of all the groups involved were used for analysis

Result and discussion for Step 1 Comparing the descriptives computed for each rater, it was found that the means (5.118 and 5.823 for pre-mean, and 9.010 and 8.896 for post-mean) and standard deviation (2.694 and 2.936 for pre-total scores, and 3.297 and 2.962 for post-total scores) were very close, while both skewness and kurtosis were insignificant in their effect in every instance. These initial findings suggested that the two sets of ratings stood a good chance of being consistent in their ratings.

Step 2 The Spearman Rank-Order Correlation Coefficients between two total ratings were calculated both for the pre-total score as well as the post-total score using the designated formula (Bachman, 1990:180). The higher the coefficients, the more reliable are the two ratings.

Results and discussion for Step 2 The results were extremely encouraging. With a correlation coefficient of 0.915 for the pre-total score, and 0.832 for the post-total score, it was legitimate to claim with confidence that the two ratings had a strong correlation and hence the scale itself could be considered reliable.

Development of measurement scale for evaluating self-direction

The second rating scale was developed to measure another key construct under study – self-direction. Theoretically, self-direction refers to a learner's ability to take charge of, self-organise or manage her own learning process (Dickinson, 1987; Holec, 1996). To measure this construct, it has also been operationally defined as 'the learners' ability to set realistic goals for their learning, identify scope of learning (listening skills or sub-skills and strategies in this present study), relevant materials to work with and related activities to engage in, and skilfully employ them for monitoring their own learning, set their own pace for learning, and conduct self-assessment'. In concrete terms, learners are expected to be able to further conduct their learning by setting realistic, specific long-term and short-term goals (on completion of an initial course such as the one designed for this study); identifying relevant materials and skills, sub-skills or strategies to practise; engaging in appropriate activities to enhance learning; adopting a specific approach to proceed with personal learning, and conducting self-assessment throughout the process.

Background To elicit this construct, learners were invited to design a personal course for self-directed language learning covering all the aspects of self-direction as defined above. This 'personal course design' was meant to be a comprehensive device to elicit both the individual learner's conceptual under-standing (metacognitive awareness) of various aspects of self-directed language learning, and their actual ability (methodological techniques) in planning for such mode of learning. While the ability to produce a 'perfect' personal course design for self-directed language learning will not necessarily guarantee its successful implementation, we can nevertheless infer from a conceptual representation of the course, in the form of a course design, whether a learner has grasped the rationale behind it, or has the potential and/or ability to do so.

This conceptual understanding is crucial for 'true' self-directed learning. Brookfield asserts that in understanding the concept of self-direction, 'we cannot conceive self-direction solely in terms of a command of self-instructional techniques'. This is because, it may be 'possible to be a superb technician of self-directed learning in terms of one's command of goal setting, instructional design or evaluative procedures, and yet to exercise no critical questioning of the validity or worth of one's intellectual pursuit as compared with competing, alternative possibilities' (Brookfield, 1985:29, cited in Candy, 1991:19-20).

In this connection, Candy speaks of two kinds of autonomy: situational and epistemological, which learners should attain in order to be fully self-directed.

In brief, situational autonomy refers to the technical engineering of learning tasks, while epistemological autonomy refers to a higher level of cognitive control with a high degree of meta-cognitive awareness and self-monitoring (Candy, 1991:414).

In enhancing self-directed language learning, it is autonomous learners who are both practically and cognitively in control of their personal learning that we ultimately aim to develop, not robot learners who mechanically carry out all designated activities without much meta-cognitive awareness of their overall learning process. Therefore, this meta-cognitive awareness, which enhances a learner's overall understanding of the rationale behind all her actions and self-management of the entire learning process, must be developed in enhancing self-directed language learning. By definition, the concept implies a raising of the learner's level of control from the immediate task level to that of a more perspectivised awareness, with overall process control. This should work in the service of self-direction. For this reason, it can be argued that meta-cognitive or critically reflective ability is a necessary condition for conducting self-directed learning, the process of which entails both the planning and implementation of the design in creative and flexible ways.

On the basis of such assumptions, it was taken as likely that meta-cognitive awareness or epistemological knowledge would be reflected in the personal course design in terms of overall coherence and relatedness among all items concerned, if they were well managed as a whole. This explains why many of the criteria set for item evaluation pertain to notions of relevance and coherence which would be seen as indications of the operation of higher and abstract levels of process control.

Identification of items for evaluation In order to strengthen construct validity of measurement, a framework outlining the various headings was provided for each learner to work with. As mentioned, all the item headings reflect or represent different aspects or components of the key construct under study. It is worth noting that no specific guidelines or criteria for judgement were provided. Such information was deliberately withdrawn to avoid a modelling effect. However, students were informed of what each heading meant and were encouraged to be creative and personal in design.

To help students produce a personal course design, the following framework was given, anticipating input for specific aspects or components of conducting self-directed learning[1]: long-term goals; short-term goals; choice of materials; skills to practise; activities to engage in*; types or amount of assignments*; approach to take*; (i.e. how to implement their study plan, addressing the mode of learning, how often and where); form of assessment.

This framework, though it seems to have separate and discrete headings for consideration, forms a coherent whole aiming to represent learners' overall perception of how they could be in control of their own learning process. It starts with personal needs analysis which is intended to result in setting specific and realistic goals. To achieve their perceived goals, learners would need to identify specific skills and strategies to learn or practice; select relevant materials to work with; and choose the activities to engage in. They would also need to set related tasks or assignments for continuous learning. More importantly, they had to set criteria for assessment, in particular, self-assessment. Relevance and coherence were of prime importance throughout the design process. An examination of all the items included would show how they are related to one another. For example, if one's goal is to understand informal conversational exchanges spoken at a normal speed, one would need to select materials or genres that provide such listening opportunities as in comedies, movies, or phone-in programmes. Listening to formal news programmes would not be directly conducive to achieving one's goal. This kind of implicit relatedness and overall coherence is built into the design and is clearly reflected in the criteria for rating.

The scale and scoring details To measure the impact the treatment has had on learners' self-direction, a rating scale comprising 17 items was developed to evaluate each learner's personal course designs produced both at the beginning and at the end of the course. Three independent raters were invited to read through all the entries of personal course design and evaluate their *adequacy*, *usefulness* and *coherence* by rating all the aspects covered in the each entry.

A seven-point rating scale (0 to 6) was used to determine the degree to which each statement was reflective of each aspect under evaluation. On this rating scale, 1 was used to indicate that the aspect mentioned definitely did not apply or that there was no basis for judgement, whereas 6 definitely applied. 0 referred to cases where no such aspect was covered. Raters were requested to circle their choice on the scale (Figure 1). To minimise personal bias and inconsistency, detailed notes for raters were prepared, and a brief training session held to acquaint raters with crucial criterial pointers.

Discussion As implicated by the previous discussion, relevance of selected items on the list was often a function of how other items were defined. Overall coherence of the entire personal course design was an implicit feature highlighted throughout, though it was only made explicit in the last two items.

Validation of the measurement scale for self-direction A measurement scale is useful if and only if it is reliable. Reliability is defined by Kirk and Miller as 'the extent to which a measurement procedure yields the same answer however and whenever it is carried out' (1986:19). In other words, it is the degree to which

Figure I The seven-point rating scale used for evaluation

Please circle your choice 0 = Definitely not 6 = Definitely yes

I The long-term goal(s) is/are relevant	0 1 2 3 4 5 6
2 The long-term goal(s) is/are specific	0 1 2 3 4 5 6
3 The short-term goal(s) is/are relevant	0 1 2 3 4 5 6
4 The short-term goal(s) is/are specific	0 1 2 3 4 5 6
5 The short-term goal(s) is/are realist	0 1 2 3 4 5 6
6 The materials chosen are specific	0 1 2 3 4 5 6
7 The materials chosen are adequate	0 1 2 3 4 5 6
8 The materials chosen are relevant to achieving the goals	0 1 2 3 4 5 6
9 The skills to practise are specific	0 1 2 3 4 5 6
10 The skills to practise are conducive to achieving the goals	0 1 2 3 4 5 6
11 The activities to engage in are conducive to achieving the goals	0 1 2 3 4 5 6
12 The types of assignments are conducive to achieving the goals	0 1 2 3 4 5 6
13 The approach is specific enough to proceed with personal learning	0 1 2 3 4 5 6
14 The forms for overall assessment are defined specifically	0 1 2 3 4 5 6
15 The forms of assessment has included or implied criteria for conducting self-assessment	0 1 2 3 4 5 6
16 The personal course design has internal coherence	0 1 2 3 4 5 6
17 The personal course design is practicable	0 1 2 3 4 5 6

the finding is independent of accidental circumstances of the research. To ensure reliability of measurements, two facets of the generalisability study, namely the internal consistency of items, and inter-rater consistency need to be addressed.

Internal consistency of items Prior to adopting this rating scale, rigorous statistical procedures were carried out to ensure the internal consistency of items of the whole scale. Scorings of the researcher for all the entries (66 for pre-test and 55 for post-test) were subjected to the 'Guttman Odd-Even Split Half' analysis for the reliability coefficients for both rating scales. Guttman's model was identified mainly for its robustness in data analysis.

Computing reliability coefficients Relevant data for both ratings were input and analysed using SPSS, a statistical package for the social sciences. Running of the data showed the following descriptions and results.[2]

Findings and discussion for reliability analysis for the pre-test rating scale

1   Statistics for both part 1 and part 2 showed that they were roughly 'equal halves' with similar total means (9.7879 and 7.7121) and item means (1.3983 and 1.1017). The variance means, though not closely similar, could be considered acceptable (1.6007 and 0.9228 respectively).

2   All items were found to be fit to be retained for rating purposes because the alpha for each item if deleted were all high with a range of 0.9112 to 0.9231.

3   The internal consistency among all items was calculated and found to be very high, with a Guttman Split-Half Alpha of 0.9409.

4   The entire pre-test rating scale of 14 items was found to have a very high internal consistency among items.

Findings and discussion for reliability analysis for the post-test rating scale

1   Statistics for both part 1 and part 2 showed that they were 'equal halves' with similar total means (30.2727 and 26.1455 respectively), item means (3.3636 and 3.2682 respectively) and item variance means (2.7348 and 3.0238 respectively).

2   All items were found to be fit to be retained for rating purposes because the alpha for each item if deleted were all high with a range of 0.9226 to 0.9373.

3   The internal consistency among all items was calculated and found to be high with a Guttman Split-Half Alpha of 0.9707.

4   The entire post-test rating scale of 17 items was found to have very high internal consistency among items.

Inter-rater reliability

Three independent raters were invited to evaluate both versions of the personal course design using pre-test and post-test rating scales respectively. To minimise personal bias and inconsistency in rating, raters' notes were prepared for each rater in addition to the training session provided before their own attempt. Raw scores from the three independent raters were input to calculate Spearman Rank-Order Correlation Coefficients among their ratings. Analysis of the data showed statistics for each rater as per the following (Table 5).

Table 5 Summary statistics for raters 1 – 3 on both rating scales

Variable	Mean	Std Dev	Min	Max	Valid N
pretot1	17.50	11.14	.00	36.00	66 (Rater 1)
pretot2	18.41	11.93	.00	41.00	66 (Rater 2)
pretot3	20.41	12.75	.00	47.00	66 (Rater 3)

Key: pretot = total score for the pre-test, the number following shows the rater

postot1	56.34	19.85	27.00	99.00	56 (Rater 1)
postot2	48.60	19.18	18.00	93.00	55 (Rater 2)
postot3	49.73	17.39	22.00	94.00	56 (Rater 3)

Key: postot = total score for the post-test, the number following shows the rater

premean1	1.25	.80	.00	2.57	66 (Rater 1)
premean2	1.31	.85	.00	2.93	66 (Rater 2)
premean3	1.46	.91	.00	3.36	66 (Rater 3)

Key: premean = mean score per item for the pre-test, the number following shows the rater

posmean1	3.34	1.17	1.59	5.82	56 (Rater 1)
posmean2	2.86	1.13	1.06	5.47	55 (Rater 2)
posmean3	2.93	1.02	1.29	5.53	56 (Rater 3)

Key: posmean = mean score per item for the post-test, the number following shows the rater

pretot	18.77	11.52	00.00	39.33	66 (Raters 1,2,3)
postot	51.45	17.33	22.67	95.33	56 (Raters 1,2,3)

Key: pretot = composite total mean score based on all three raters for the pre-test
posmean = composite total mean score based on all three raters for the pre-test

To determine the reliability coefficients among the three raters, the designated formula for calculating Spearman Rank-Order Coefficients was used (Bachman, 1990:180). It was found that the coefficients calculated for both ratings were pleasingly high: 0.96 and 0.92 for the pre-test scores and the post-test scores respectively.

Results and discussion

1   As calculated above, the Spearman Rank-Order Coefficients for both rating scales were found to be very high, with 0.96 for the pre-test scores and 0.92 for the post-test scores.
2   Based on the above findings, it could be said with confidence that the inter-rater reliability among all three ratings for both rating scales was very high. A detailed examination of the pre-mean scores (premeans) and the post-mean scores (posmeans) and standard deviation (Std Dev)

among all raters would support the above claim. They were all so close that one would hardly expect otherwise.

3   Therefore, the mean scores obtained from three raters for each learner could also be claimed as highly reliable.

Conclusion

With the high internal consistency of items found among the rating scale for process control, and the highly positive findings about the inter-rater reliability for the rating scale for self-direction, it could be claimed with confidence that the two rating scales under consideration were both valid and reliable. Correspondingly, this permitted the confident claim that the composite scores calculated based on the total mean scores of various raters were meaningful and reliable. ▓

Acknowledgements

I feel greatly indebted to Professor Lyle Bachman who has given me great insights and support in conducting this study.

Notes

1   Learners were invited to produce a personal course design both before and after the course. Aspects with an asterisk (*) were excluded in the requirement set for the pre-course personal course design. They were excluded on the grounds that learners found those aspects totally unfamiliar and hence impossible to provide any input. To encourage input, they were left out of the initial attempt so that students could concentrate on other items with which they felt more comfortable.
2   Statistics tables for both rating scales are obtainable from the author upon request.

References

Bachman, L.F. (1990) *Fundamental Consideration in Language Testing*. Oxford: Oxford University Press.
Bailey, K.M. (1998) *Learning about Language Assessment: dilemmas, direction and decisions*. Boston: Heinle and Heinle.
Candy, P. (1991) *Self-direction for Lifelong Learning: a comprehensive guide to theory and practice*. San Francisco, California: Jossey-Bass.
Dickinson, L. (1987) *Self-instruction in Language Learning*. Cambridge: Cambridge University Press.
Holec, H. (1981) *Autonomy and Foreign Language Learning*. Strasbourg: Council of Europe.
Holec, H. (1996) Self-directed learning: an alternative form of training. In H. Holec, D. Little and R. Richterich.
Holec, H., Little, D. and Richterich, R. (1996) *Strategies in Language Learning and Use: studies towards a common European framework of reference for language learning and teaching*. Germany: Council of Europe Publishing.
Kirk, J. and Miller, M.C. (1986) *Reliability and Validity in Qualitative Research*. Beverly Hills: SAGE Publications.
Little, D. (1991) *Learner Autonomy 1: definitions, issues and problems*. Dublin: Authentik.
Little, D. (1996) Freedom to learn and compulsion to interact. In R. Pemberton et al. (eds) *Taking Control: autonomy in language learning*. Hong Kong: Hong Kong University Press.
Shavelson, R.J. (1996) *Statistical Reasoning for the Behavioural Sciences*. USA: Allyn and Bacon.
Wenden, A. (1988) A Curricular Framework for Promoting Learner Autonomy. *Canadian Modern Language Review*, 44:639-52.
Wenden, A. (1991) *Learner Strategies for Learner Autonomy*. London: Prentice Hall International.
Willing, K. (1989a) *Teaching How to Learn: learning strategies in ESL*. Teacher's guide. Sydney: National Centre for English Language Teaching and Research (NCELTR) Macquarie University.
Willing, K. (1989b) *Teaching How to Learn: learning strategies in ESL. Activity worksheets*. Sydney: National Centre for English Language Teaching and Research (NCELTR) Macquarie University.

◆ The assessment of learner autonomy and language learning

◆ Evaluation de l'autonomie et apprentissage des langues

Marie-France Champagne, Terry Clayton,
Nicholas Dimmitt, Matthew Laszewski,
William Savage, Jonathan Shaw, Richmond Stroupe,
Myint Myint Thein and Pierre Walter
Asian Institute of Technology (AIT), Thailand

Abstract
An action research project by a group of faculty colleagues working as teacher-researchers culminates in qualitative and quantitative measures to assess learners' engagement of their autonomy and the improvement of their language capability through an experiential educational approach. The project begins by reviewing conceptualisations of task, autonomy and language as these have been informed by practitioner-researchers in various disciplines, and developed over 14 years in the AIT Centre for Language and Educational Technology. During the first phase of this year-long study, tasks on our pre-masters program called Talkbase are described, as are their autonomy and language objectives. During the second, assessment measures are designed and piloted, and in the third, implemented and evaluated. The paper problematises and addresses the inter-dependent issues of how learner autonomy can be assessed, and how the learning of language can be measured in a manner consistent with a critical pedagogy that explicitly promotes learner autonomy.

Résumé
Un groupe d'enseignants-chercheurs mène un projet de recherche-action sur un programme de langue utilisant une approche expérientielle. Cette recherche aboutit au développement d'instruments de mesure qualitative et quantitative pour évaluer le degré d'autonomie des apprenants, ainsi que leurs acquis langagiers. Les notions de tâche, d'autonomie et d'apprentissage de la langue ne sont pas nouvelles et ont été définies de

différentes manières selon les disciplines. La recherche fait le point sur ces différents concepts et décrit leur évolution au sein même du Centre de Langues et de Technologies Educatives de l'AIT lors de la dernière décennie. Ce projet d'un an se déroule en trois phases: durant la première, les tâches utilisées dans Talkbase – le programme pré-Mastère étudié – sont décrites, puis des méthodes d'évaluation sont conçues et testées, pour enfin être mises en place et évaluées lors de la dernière étape. Cet article s'attache à analyser les questions interdépendantes de l'évaluation de l'autonomie de l'apprenant et de la mesure de son apprentissage de la langue tout en respectant les exigences d'une pédagogie critique qui promeut l'autonomie.

Introduction

More than a year after we wrote this abstract, we now read it as a plan. It was our intention to develop both qualitative and quantitative measures to assess learner autonomy and language improvement and to proceed in a sequence of phases. From the abstract, we developed an outline of the intended project and assigned ourselves sections as co-authors.

Talkbase is the only program in our centre on which all of us have taught. In our collegial context (Hall and Kenny, 1995), we have always spent a good deal of time discussing what happens in our classrooms and considering different ways of doing things. This first centre-wide research and writing project has afforded the current faculty an opportunity to reflect on and understand more clearly how we each perceive what the program and our centre approach are about. In retrospect, what we have found in this year-long effort is that we have been engaged in an exploratory study. We are negotiating issues that are fundamental to what learner autonomy might be within our particular language learning context. The purpose of this paper has thus become to document how far we have progressed toward our intended purpose in the original abstract, and to account for how we have seen that purpose change.

The first section briefly describes how constructs of language, task and autonomy have been conceptualised into working definitions in our centre and on Talkbase, which has become a 'laboratory' for this research. Two following sections on the interdependent issues of assessing language and autonomy distil the essence of our discussions over a series of ten research round-table sessions, and over putting this paper together. This continues in the fourth section which reports on outcomes of our action research. The paper closes with what we have learned.

Language, task and autonomy

Talkbase began in 1985 as a pre-masters language program in the then English Language centre at AIT. As we came to understand the role of language and communication in our educational and development context, so too have we come to realise that our programs were doing more for students than enabling them to use language better. A complete picture of that context, and Talkbase's approach, framework and tasks, have been described by present and former colleagues (Hall and Kenny, 1988; Kenny, 1993a, b; Savage, 1994; Thein, 1994; Clayton and Shaw, 1997; Kenny and Laszewski, 1997; Walter, 1998).

Training and education, product and process, form and content, learner-
and teacher-centred, static and dynamic, exercise and task. Such have been the
dichotomous limits of our discussions over a decade and a half, as we also came
to understand that we should be trying to describe our approach to language
education, not in terms of dichotomies, but rather continua. Likewise, we have
struggled with describing what is happening on our programs beyond the
learning of language. Is it educational potential, interaction, critical awareness,
experience, investigative research, autonomy?

In a review of Widdowson's (1983) *Learning Purpose and Language Use*,
Kenny (1985) wrote about language being put to use, taking on meaning (as
the content of communication) in subject areas other than language-for-itself,
and reinforcing and developing learners' interests in an authentic and
motivating content. Another early article (Hall et al., 1986a) described the
centre as 'not hav[ing] a body of knowledge of its own to impart' (p. 59) but
rather responding to situational needs. They also stressed, and we continue to
remind ourselves, that '[the] notion of "testing" … must be seen in this
context' (p.59) and that tests must 'fit in with our overall educational
philosophy, and … that this compatibility must always be essential in any
curriculum' (p.67).

Our approach to the learning and teaching of language rests on particular
understandings of knowledge, content and meaning. The task is our
methodological unit of practice, with implications for teacher and learner
roles. By framing the approach in terms of experiential learning, we are able to
realise a particular expression of learner autonomy.

The approach depends on the use and generation of knowledge (Hall and
Kenny, 1988:28) by our learner-participants, the content they provide
(Laszewski, 1989:69) and the work we do with them so they can handle it
better. Learner content is defined to be 'that which interests and motivates
them, informed by their own subjectivity' (Shaw, 1991:110). Since we all arrive
in any educational context with our own subjective realities, we can only
begin to understand each other, and the work we have to do together, by
negotiating what we mean by what we say and want to say (Hall et al.,
1986b:149; Hall and Kenny, 1988:19).

The practice of autonomy and language learning is realised through tasks,
which we define broadly, while maintaining common characteristics across
them. '[Tasks] are derived from and defined by actual work [and study]
situations in which the learner needs to use English' (Savage and Storer,
1992:195; Savage and Whisenand, 1993). Initial tasks are teacher-defined (Hall
and Kenny, 1988:23) and must 'be appropriately set up so that, on reporting
back, language and content are generated to allow the participants to proceed'
(Savage and Storer, 1992:195). In any program or workshop, there is a
deliberate movement 'from teacher-defined tasks to tasks identified by the
participants themselves' (Savage and Storer, 1992:191). Finally, tasks are to be
distinguished from exercises in that they must 'be perceived by the learners as
embodying meanings of their own' (Kenny, 1993b:225).

For autonomy to be realised, teacher and learner roles must be redefined,
for not doing so, or not seeing any reason to, may be a barrier to achieving the

strong version of autonomous learning we are putting forward. Hall and Kenny (1988:22) write about teachers 'bring[ing] students to the point where they are willing to offer and receive criticism'; Laszewski (1989:72) talks about teachers guiding students in their development, with all recognising that 'a guide cannot pass on the development he [or she] has attained as a substitute for the learner's own'. An excerpt from Kenny captures our conceptualisation of learner autonomy:

> Autonomy is not just a matter of permitting choice in learning situations, or making pupils responsible for the activities they undertake, but of allowing and encouraging learners, through processes deliberately set up for the purpose, to begin to express who they are, what they think, and what they would like to do, in terms of work they initiate and define for themselves. (Kenny, 1993a:440)

We have grown to view this definition as akin to those found in the experiential learning literature, such as:

> Learning is the process whereby knowledge is created through the transformation of experience. Knowledge results from the combination of grasping experience and transforming it. (Kolb, 1984:1)

Assessing language

Given the concepts that underpin the approach, Talkbase is much more than a language program. Talkbase participants are a diverse bunch who include mature bureaucrats, aspiring technocrats and fresh college graduates. Some have had little prior exposure to English in or out of school; some have had several years of English classes but have never used the language for their own purposes; some have completed English-medium undergraduate programs. The program 'has its origin in what was seen as a pedagogic need rather than in any particular language-teaching theory' (Hall and Kenny, 1988:20), a need that reflected what the participants' previous language education lacked: developing the confidence and ability to use their existing knowledge to fulfil effectively the requirements of their degree program. Language teaching at AIT has continued to evolve from a remediation of linguistic and pedagogic needs into maintenance of an environment in which we seek to bring students' thoughts out in the open, as a step towards developing their communicative abilities and towards allowing and encouraging their autonomy.

Data on language learning are generated by participants in response to program tasks listed below. Most of these data come from what Brown and Hudson (1998) characterise as 'personal-response' assessments, those which 'allow students to communicate what they want to communicate' (p. 663), as opposed to more structured forms of assessment in which communication and performance are restricted to a finite realm of possibilities pre-established by teacher-testers. In assessing participant progress for pedagogical purposes, Talkbase teachers have depended on 'personal-response' measures such as portfolios of work and participants' self-perceptions of progress together with teacher observations. Sources for language learning data on Talkbase have included:

- Entry-exit interviews and self-assessment

- Portfolios of work (individual and group)
  written and graphical work
  audio tapes made outside the classroom
  video tapes made outside the classroom
  computer-based presentations
  pieces of work

- Teacher observations of progress
  report-backs
  individual consultations
  field trip
  classroom videotapes

- Participant self-perceptions of progress
  reflection-on-action and evaluations
  journals
  writing feedback sessions

For purposes of program accountability, however, tests seem to be the most accepted evidence of second language acquisition, with test scores more likely to satisfy administrators and funders. Testing has in fact been a considerable topic of debate and experimentation among Talkbase teachers over several years. Some say the tests provide at least a replicable measure of second language acquisition, and should be designed to reflect the types of tasks used in the program. Others maintain that the tests they have used on Talkbase, such as 'C-tests', can be designed to capture both ESP and general language competence, regardless of the pedagogy employed (Connelly, 1997). Still others have argued that any standardised test such as IELTS would show the same results. And some of us maintain that if the results of the tests are discussed with students in the negotiation of program objectives and as a means of making language acquisition a conscious process, this will enhance language learning. Finally, there are those who believe that testing itself is anti-autonomy, serving to reinforce (on the crucial first and last days of the participants' experience on the program) traditional notions of teacher control and student accountability. Even when discussions of test results are integrated into the curriculum, this focuses attention on language itself as the subject of learner inquiry, and works against learners being autonomous in identifying content of interest to them.

Assessing autonomy

In defining autonomy, Kenny (1993a), Savage (1997) and Pennycook (1997) have taken the idea of autonomy as learner control (Benson, 1997; Holec, 1987; Nunan, 1997) and expanded it to embrace the concept of self-realisation, of learners finding a voice in English and becoming 'authors of their own worlds' (Pennycook, 1997:45). On Talkbase, we thus have to speak of assessing how learners 'express who they are, what they think, and what they would like to do, in terms of the work they initiate and define for themselves' (Kenny, 1993a:440). We can take a rich collection of data on learner autonomy from three sources: a) learners' work (portfolios of written and graphical work, video and audio-tapes they make outside the classroom, presentations of pieces of work); b) our observations (in report-back sessions, interviews, classroom videotapes); and c) participants' self-perceptions of progress (in their journals, oral and written evaluations).

In the first instance, portfolios of work show us, through the content learners choose to investigate in-depth, something of who they are, what they think and what they would like to do. In deciding on topics for pieces of work, planning and undertaking field work and presenting what they have learned, participants are not only directing themselves, but clearly expressing who they are. In the process, they typically alternate between depression and elation, despair and excitement, enthusiasm and ennui, extreme pride in what they have done and loathing of the whole thing. These human emotions are indicative of participant engagement with their work (and with autonomy). Emotions are also present, but not as tangibly or visibly, when learners undertake teacher-directed tasks in the beginning of the program.

Second, our observations and records (notes, videos and teacher discussions) of report-back sessions capture narratives of work outside the classroom, where participants are free to do whatever they want in carrying out tasks. These narratives generally move from conventional and safe learning strategies (consult a dictionary, go to the library, talk to a friend) to more adventurous self-directed learning (visit a laboratory, consult the Internet, interview strangers and experts) as the program progresses, again indicating some measure of learner autonomy at work. Report-backs also give us the opportunity to observe how participants work in terms of autonomy goals and objectives outlined in the next section of this paper, for example, how they reflect on and use personal experience, locate and use information resources, and critically examine their own and others' work.

Finally, learners' self-perceptions of their progress are also taken as indicators of autonomy. Personal journals give us valuable insights into how participants perceive their own learning evolving toward autonomy through the program. Writers talk about the difficulties and challenges of learning on their own, sometimes for the first time; and about how they understand the pedagogy promoting autonomy. In oral and written evaluations in the first and last weeks, participants also often comment on their personal involvement with pieces of work, how they have never worked so hard in their lives, how they feel confident as independent adult learners. Three excerpts from learners' written evaluations illustrate these sentiments:

> A piece of work, something that we have a new experience, in deciding topic, deciding what we will do and organising some works with team work. By this way, we can see the real world, see the process of a factory, to see what is the problem that factory found and try to get a solution to solve that problem.

For the method of teaching is quite new for me, of course at the beginning was quite difficult for everyone in our class because we didn't know what the aim of our teacher was. But later we understood that they tried to teach us to be on our own. It like the proverb 'teach people how to fish, better than give them a fish.'

The teacher didn't teach me about these things – I learnt it from friend, from myself. It seem a good method to encourage students' effort to discover the unknown.

Language and autonomy on Talkbase

To help us formulate this action-research project, we invited Richard Schmidt (Department of ESL, University of Hawai'i at Manoa) to be a participant-observer for a couple of weeks on Talkbase and to advise us on how we might assess language acquisition. His eventual suggestions were to look at confidence, autonomy, fluency, academic discourse, vocabulary and global proficiency. For example, fluency might be indicated by counting words per minute (and disfluency by number of false starts), vocabulary by type-token ratio, confidence and autonomy through student journals, and discourse by analysing a tape of a group at work.

Goals and objectives Schmidt's first query was whether we had a statement of Talkbase program objectives. Because it seems obvious that any assessment would be done against objectives, from that opening query, a lot of work has gone into reviewing, debating, and revising the objectives. A list of Talkbase objectives had been drafted in the early 1990s from a similar set of stimuli that were used in the late 1980s for participants to self-assess themselves on program goals. As we came to understand the importance of being more explicit with the participants about our approach, in the first week of the program, they were given the hand-out shown (Figure 1), which was discussed in a whole group session.

Figure 1 The hand-out used to stimulate discussion for Talkbase goals

---

Some Talkbase objectives

These are some of the things we hope participants will do better as a result of the Talkbase workshop:

> Initiate pieces of work
> Plan, organise and carry out pieces of work
> Be able to explain why they are doing what they are doing
> Be able to understand what other people mean when they talk
> and write about what they are doing
> Examine their own work critically
> Clarify ideas in speech and in writing
> Use media in the process of clarifying ideas and carrying out pieces of work
> Elicit relevant information from other people
> Work and cooperate with other people

What are your objectives?

For the current project, several of us worked together to develop distinct goals and objectives for learner autonomy and for language proficiency. On the assumption that we should be assessing language and autonomy separately, we tried to sort them out and felt the need to rework the original list. Through this process, two sets of goals and two sets of objectives were developed, as shown in Figure 2.

Figure 2 Talkbase goals and objectives

Learner autonomy goals	Language proficiency goals
Understand why you are doing what you are doing	Understand what others mean when they talk and write about what they are doing
Become a self-directed learner, both alone and within groups	Negotiate meaning
Make connections between classroom learning and the world beyond	
Reflect on and use personal experience	
Engage in new experiences outside the AIT campus	

Learner autonomy objectives	Language proficiency objectives
Locate and use information resources	Increase knowledge of relevant vocabulary
Elicit relevant information from others	Engage with academic and research discourse conventions
Critically examine your own and others' work	
Initiate, plan, organise and carry out a piece of work	Clarify and present ideas in speech and in writing
	Explain why you are doing what you are doing

The criterion for distinguishing goals from objectives was that objectives, but not goals, could be assessed. Distinguishing goals and objectives for autonomy from those for language was not found to be as straightforward. For example, 'elicit relevant information from others' was regarded by some as clearly indicative of autonomous learning, but its relevance for language proficiency is undeniable. It became clear that the lists are interrelated. Looking at goals and objectives in the context of a task makes this even clearer.

Language and autonomy in an interview task
In identifying their own fields of interest, participants conduct a series of interviews with researchers on our campus. They go out and choose who they will interview. They also decide whether to record their interviews on a cassette tape or video and choose one of their interviews to play back for the whole group the next day. This task gives them opportunities to locate sources

of information (people) and to elicit relevant information from them. To report back to the group on what was done, they have to clarify and present their ideas as well as their motives.

One recent participant treated this task as an exercise and asked a string of questions, not related to each other and not all relevant to the interviewee. The motivation he gave for his approach to the task was that he assumed the teachers expected a long interview. A pair of students handled the same interview task quite differently. They selected a newly-graduated student in their own field of study and interviewed him on videotape about manufacturing resource planning, re-engineering concepts and materials management, three areas related to his own field. They were able to get him to illustrate his research by joining him for a tour of the industrial engineering laboratories.

The experience of doing an interview provides fertile ground for working toward the above goals and objectives. The two examples given highlight differences between self-directed learning and acting to fulfil teacher expectations as well as the difference between eliciting relevant information and eliciting information for its own sake. The subsequent task of reporting back on why they did what they did, which is related to a language objective, prompts consideration of the personal and social relevance of their work.

Assessing, measuring or reflecting? Keeping various assessment options in mind, and depending on sources of data integral to the program, we tried several measures which could be assessed quantitatively. On the first of the two most recent Talkbase programs, teachers experimented with dictations as an objective measure of language proficiency, listening comprehension and accuracy. Although the dictation results showed improvement in all three areas, teachers felt that the dictations, compared to performance in interviews, journal entries, presentations of pieces of work, and discussions, were reductionist and trivial. Quantitative assessment of writing showed that some participants made gains in grammatical accuracy. We also saw clear evidence of language improvement in terms of the confidence with which they expressed their ideas and the fluency with which they conversed and wrote in English.

On the most recent Talkbase, we placed an emphasis on participant self-assessment. Building on our experience with an innovation introduced earlier in the year, we asked students to reflect on action (i.e., to describe what they had been doing over a period of time and to assess their performance and that of the group). This led to an assessment of Talkbase, its approach, methods and tasks. It also led to students declaring whether and to what extent they were making gains in language proficiency. Three reflection-on-action sessions at the end of the first, fourth, and eighth weeks were timetabled before the start of the program. A few impromptu sessions also took place after completion of work which students seemed to find particularly satisfying. At the end of week one, students commented on how the program was unexpected, but a welcome change from other language programs they had been on. After week four, they remarked on their improvement in language, particularly with understanding each other and the teachers. A participant-defined organisational structure for all the presentations was noted by the teachers. During the final session in week eight, participants commented on how much they valued being on the program, but differed as to whether the first or second half was more important. During the final open-house presentation, participants were clearly impressed by the seriousness of the questions posed by people they perceived to be experienced in their fields of study.

In conclusion: what we have learned

To take a pro-autonomy approach through to its logical conclusion, we have learned that we need to be moving towards self-assessment by participants of their own progress. We acknowledge, however, that in such a move away from conventionally accepted, quantifiable measures, we must ensure that methods for self-assessment, and its data analysis, are rigorous, a recent call similarly made for verbal report data in language learning strategies research (Cohen, 1998:56). Any data to be used for assessment (or teacher-research for that matter) should already be an integral part of the program. We must maintain an integrity around the compatibility of testing with an educational approach that aims to be pro-autonomy. Having said that, we can continue to explore ways of demonstrating quantifiable improvement of participants' language proficiency by analysing data from several of the sources we have identified.

What we have also learned from this year of even-more-than-usual discussions about our work, is the importance of an emerging field of inquiry among our learner autonomy colleagues, that of teacher autonomy (Coyle et al., 2000). Perhaps this is the way through our disparate understandings of what autonomy is, by looking back at ourselves as learners and reflecting on that experience as we ask our own participants to experience what we think is learner autonomy. Certainly within our centre, this has been revealing in our differences over issues of testing, qualitative-quantitative, goals-objectives. We demand a great deal of program participants when we ask them to strive towards our definitions of learner autonomy, this made especially clear when we reflect on whether we allow it to happen among ourselves as teacher and researcher colleagues. ■

References

Benson, P. (1997) The philosophy and politics of learner autonomy. In P. Benson and P. Voller, (eds) *Autonomy and Independence in Language Learning.* Essex: Addison Wesley Longman.

Brown, J. D. and Hudson, T. (1998) The alternatives in language assessment. *TESOL Quarterly,* 32,4:653-75.

Clayton, T. and Shaw, J. (1997) Discovering resources in Ho Chi Minh City. In B. Kenny and W. Savage (eds) *Language and Development: teachers in a changing world.* Essex: Addison Wesley Longman.

Cohen, A. D. (1998) *Strategies in Learning and Using a Second Language.* Essex: Addison Wesley Longman.

Connelly, M. (1997) Using C-tests in English with post-graduate students. *English for Specific Purposes,* 16,2:139-50.

Coyle, D., Lamb, T., McGrath, I. and Sinclair, B. (eds) (2000) *Learner Autonomy, Teacher Autonomy: future directions.* Essex: Addison Wesley Longman.

Hall, D., Hawkey, R. and Kenny, B. (1986a) Testing student language performance at the Asian Institute of Technology. *Pasaa,* 16,2:60-8.

Hall, D., Hawkey, R., Kenny, B. and Storer, G. (1986b) Patterns of thought in scientific writing: a course in information structuring for engineering students. *English for Specific Purposes,* 5,2:147-60.

Hall, D. and Kenny, B. (1988) An approach to a truly communicative methodology: the AIT pre-sessional course. *English for Specific Purposes,* 7,1:19-32.

Hall, D. and Kenny, B. (1995) Thailand: evolution of a language centre: pursuing autonomy in a collegial context. In A. Pincas (ed.) *Spreading English: ELT projects in international development.* London: Phoenix ELT.

Holec, H. (1987) The learner as manager: managing learning or managing to learn? In Wenden, A. and Rubin, J. (eds) *Learner Strategies in Language Learning.* London: Prentice Hall International.

Kenny, B. (1985) Review of Learning Purpose and Language Use. *ESP Journal,* 4,2:171-9.

Kenny, B. (1993a) For more autonomy. *System,* 21,4:431-42.

Kenny, B. (1993b) Investigative research: how it changes learner status. *TESOL Quarterly,* 27,2:217-31.

Kenny, B. and Laszewski, M. (1997) Talkbase in Vientiane. In B. Kenny and W. Savage (eds) *Language and Development: teachers in a changing world.* Essex: Addison Wesley Longman.

Kolb, D. A. (1984) *Experiential Learning: experience as the source of learning and development.* Englewood Cliffs, NJ: Prentice Hall.

Laszewski, M. (1989) Teaching English: recent hearsay and heresy. *Journal of Education,* 5,3: 63-75. Bangkok: Kasetsart University.

Nunan, D. (1997) Designing and adapting materials to encourage learner autonomy. In P. Benson and P. Voller (eds) *Autonomy and independence in language learning.* Essex: Addison Wesley Longman.

Pennycook, A. (1997) Cultural alternatives and autonomy. In P. Benson and P. Voller (eds) *Autonomy and Independence in Language Learning.* Essex: Addison Wesley Longman.

Savage, W. (1994) Learner-directed video. In H. Jung and R. Vanderplank (eds) *Barriers and Bridges: media technology in language learning.* Proceedings of the 1993 CETaLL Symposium on the Occasion of the 10th AILA World Congress in Amsterdam, The Netherlands. Frankfurt: Peter Lang Verlag.

Savage, W. (1997) Review of Taking Control: autonomy in language learning. (Pemberton, R., Li, E. S. L., Or, W. W. F., and Pierson, H. D. (eds)) *Prospect,* 12(3), 64-6.

Savage, W. and Storer, G. (1992) An emergent language program framework: actively involving learners in needs analysis. *System,* 20,2:187-99.

Savage, W. and Whisenand, R. (1993) Logbooks and language learning objectives in an intensive ESP workshop. *TESOL Quarterly,* 27,4:741-6.

Shaw, J. (1991) Reappraising needs: ESP teaching strategies. In C. Pibulchol and A. Bamford (eds) *Strategies and Techniques for Students and Teachers.* Bangkok: Thai-TESOL.

Thein, M. M. (1994) A non-native English speaking teacher's response to a learner-centered program. *System,* 22,4:463-71.

Walter, P. G. (1998) Experiential learning in language education: suggestions for practice. *Prospect,* 13,1:53-67.

Widdowson, H. G. (1983) *Learning Purpose and Language Use.* Oxford: Oxford University Press.

◈ Discourse behaviour in an autonomous learning environment

◈ Conduites discursives en situation d'apprentissage autonome

Lienhard Legenhausen
University of Münster, Germany

Abstract

This paper focuses on the discourse behaviour of young learners and especially the way this behaviour develops and changes over time. Since these learners were not subjected to any explicit teaching in the traditional sense, the question arises as to what extent they learn how to sustain a conversation and to co-construct shared meanings. Furthermore, the issue of whether an institutional setting can provide rich enough input data for learners to also develop a 'sociopragmatic competence' will be addressed. The data derive from the LAALE research project (Language Acquisition in an Autonomous Learning Environment), which is based at a Danish comprehensive school. Within this project the linguistic development of a mixed-ability class was systematically observed from the beginning to the end of their school career. The conversational data reported on in this paper were elicited after 17 and 48 months of English.

Resumé

Cet article porte sur les comportements de jeunes élèves lors de leurs dialogues, ainsi qu'au développement de ces comportements au cours de leurs premières années scolaires. Puisque les élèves n'ont pas suivi d''enseignement' dans le strict sens du terme, la question se pose de savoir dans quelle mesure ils ont appris à soutenir une conversation dans une langue étrangère et à prendre part à un dialogue fonctionnel. En outre, on s'est posé la question de savoir si une salle de cours est en mesure d'offrir une ambiance linguistique si fertile que les apprenants y développent une compétence socio-pragmatique. Les données proviennent du projet de recherches LAALE (Language Acquisition in an Autonomous Learning Environment), études qui ont lieu dans une école polyvalente danoise. Dans le cadre de ce projet, le progression linguistique d'une classe entière a été observée. Du début de leur apprentissage de l'anglais jusqu'à la fin de leur scolarité, ces élèves ont suivi un enseignement autonome. Les données présentées portent sur le comportement linguistique après 17 et 48 mois d'enseignement de la langue anglaise.

Introduction

The principles of autonomous language learning have been put into practice in many parts of the world for the past 25 years or so.[1] However, when it comes to assessing the linguistic and non-linguistic learning outcomes of autonomous learning, there is a general and widely felt lack of research data. This was one of the reasons for setting up the LAALE-Project (Language Acquisition in an Autonomous Learning Environment), whose aim is to systematically observe and analyse the linguistic development of young learners who learn English as a foreign language according to the principles of autonomous learning (cf. Dam, 1995; Dam and Legenhausen, 1996).

This paper is concerned with developmental patterns of their communicative behaviour, and compares linguistic aspects of peer-to-peer talks after one year and five months of learning English with those after four years of English.

Principles and procedures of an autonomous classroom

The principles of autonomous language learning as implemented in the classroom under discussion have been fully described in Dam (1995). They include the view that:

> learner autonomy is characterised by a readiness to take charge of one's own learning in the service of one's needs and purposes. This entails a capacity and willingness to act independently and in co-operation with others, as a socially responsible person. (Bergen, 1990, quoted in Dam, 1995)

Learning is essentially seen as a process in which the learners manage to assimilate and integrate new information into their existing knowledge. This implies heavy constraints on the teachability of new concepts and of languages in general. The teacher thus dispenses with the attempt to 'teach' linguistic forms as described in the syllabus, and instead relies on the learners' ability to work out the rules of the target language themselves. The learners are trusted to acquire language through interactions with the teacher, peers and materials. One of the teacher's most important functions is to initiate and support awareness-raising processes as regards the formal structures of the target language, of communication and of the learning process itself. Classroom activities largely centre around projects in the widest sense of the word, which might include producing word-cards, designing and performing role-plays, or researching a topic of interest to the learners. Projects are mainly carried out in pairs or small groups. At the beginning of a lesson, pairs of learners also regularly engage in 'two-minute talks', in which they discuss topics of personal interest.

The learners and the data collection procedure
The class of learners from which our data were drawn was a mixed-ability class of 21 students in a Danish comprehensive school. English lessons started in the fifth grade when the learners were about 11 years old. In the first year they had two double periods per week, each lasting 90 minutes. In the following years the number of English lessons was reduced to one double period and a regular 45-minute lesson.

The data collected for this study consist of peer-to-peer talks which can be said to be an extended version of the 'two-minute talks' mentioned above. Pairs of learners were asked to talk about a topic of their own choice for about four to five minutes. In each round they had to talk twice and with different partners. In the first data collection series after 17 months of learning English (i.e. after approximately 220 hours) there was a total of 20 talks (Round I talks). Two and a half years later after about 500 hours of English, we recorded only 16 five-minute talks, because four of the students had left the class by then (Round II talks). However, the size of the two corpora is more or less identical. They both contain about 11,000 words.

Topic selection and management
The range of topics chosen by the students in the two rounds of talks was fairly similar – with free-time activities, hobbies (music, sport), holidays etc. heading the list. This is not surprising since the context and experimental set-up will largely constrain the selection of topics. However, the fact that the average number of different topics raised per talk dropped from 4.4 topics in the first round to 1.3 topics two-and-a-half years later points to a more substantial difference in task approach. The excerpts in (1) and (2) give a first impression as to the quality of interactions in the two sets of data.[2]

(1)
LA: What kind of music do you like?
M: Eh, Bryan Adams.
LA: Yes.
M: What do you like?

LA: I like Guns'n' Roses, Metallica and Bon Jovi and Ugly Kid Joe.

M: What is your favourite artist?

(Round I talks)

(2)

AM: I heard (.) a tape yesterday.

E: Yes.

AM: Ehm, Lars had the tape, and (.) ehm it was really good, I mean (?).

                                                      Yeah,

E: we went to a festival in (.) Frederiksberg (.) Festival.

AM: Yeah.

E: In, ah ehm, I can't remember when it was but (.) yes, the, the tape was
      (.) from the festival.

(Round II talks)

The first sentence in both excerpts constitutes a topic-initiating move. A large
subset of topic-initiating moves in the Round I corpus is highly recurrent, and
can be classified as stereotypical questions. They include, 'What did you do
yesterday?', 'What are your hobbies?', 'What kind of music do you like?'. They
are especially likely to occur after longer pauses, i.e. when learners have
difficulties sustaining the conversation. Compare the adjacency of pauses and
stereotypical questions in the following excerpt:

(3)

B: I have got, ehm, a Polish dictionary or something like that and
      I'm trying to learn to say 'I can't speak Polish', in Polish of course.

M: That must not be easy.

B: I don't think so. As their ehm letters is not the same way to say
      it like we do, so I have to learn before I can say all the words. (7 sec)
      What music do you like?

M: Bryan Adams and Hathaway and Michael Jackson. *What do*
      you like?

B: Oh, I like Roxette and sometimes Guns 'n' Roses and some, ah, hip
      hop songs. I don't know the names on all of them, so. Why do you like
      Michael Jackson and Hathaway and Bryan Adams?

M: I don't know. (5 sec) *What are your hobbies?*

(Round I talks)

The major strategy for topic expansion and thus also sustaining the
conversation is the mirror-image question which echoes the partner's previous
question. It can also be observed in excerpts (1) and (3).

    Since linguistic strategies for topic management – with and without
learner participation – have been analysed for quite some time now, it seems
pertinent to compare our data with previous research. Long (1981), for
example, analysed Foreigner Talk Discourse (FTD), i.e. native speaker and
learner talk, against the background of native speaker to native speaker
interactions (NS-NS). He claimed that FTD is characterised by the fact that

topics are dealt with briefly and superficially. He calculated a ratio between topic-initiating moves and topic-continuing moves (in terms of T-units) and compared his FTD results with those of native speaker interactions. The proportion between topic-initiating and topic-continuing moves showed a clear difference with – relatively speaking – far more topic-initiating moves in FTD. Native speakers talking to one another used a proportionally much greater number of topic-continuing moves. If we apply the same measure to our two learner corpora, the difference in topic treatment becomes obvious. Table 1 includes Long's statistics for comparative purposes.

Table I Topic-initiating and topic-continuing moves

	Topic-initiating	Topic-continuing	Ratio:	S
	n	n	$T_{init} : T_{contin}$	
Round I Talks	98	581	1 : 5.9	3.57
Round II Talks	36	642	1 : 17.8	10.74
FTD (Long, 1981)	50	211	1 : 4.2	3.59
NS-NS (Long, 1981)	50	606	1 : 12.1	10.33

At first glance the very fact that the Round II talks showed a higher ratio of T-continuing to T-initiating moves than even the native speaker interactions might come as a surprise.[3] However, it seems to be a consequence of the fact that the native speakers referred to by Long (1981) did not know each other when they started their talk. This means they could not draw on mutually shared knowledge and had to establish a communicative basis first before being able to elaborate on a topic.

Another result of Long's research concerns the strategies for introducing topics. The most obvious way for starting a topic – especially in FTD – is the question, which is chosen significantly more often than statements. Questions account for 96% of all topic-initiating moves in Long's FTD corpus – as opposed to only 62% in the NS-NS corpus. Table 2 shows the statistics for the class under discussion.[4]

Table 2 Topic introductions

	Totals	Questions		Statements	
		n	%	n	%
Round I Talks	98	90	91.8	8	8.2
Round II Talks	36	21	58.3	15	41.7

Similar statistics emerge for topic continuations. Here the percentage of questions drops from 53.7 in Round I to 27.6 in Round II with a corresponding rise of statements (Table 3).

Table 3 Topic continuations

	Totals	Questions		Statements	
		n	%	n	%
Round I Talks	581	312	53.7	269	46.3
Round II Talks	642	177	27.6	465	72.4

The statistics all boil down to the fact that communicatively less competent learners switch topics more often and use questions as the main strategy for introducing and developing the topic.[5]

Topic switches decrease, however, to the extent that learners manage to incorporate shared knowledge and elaborate points of mutual interest. The importance of shared knowledge in conversational exchanges has also been stressed by Cook: '...successful communication involves the transfer of information, and that transfer presupposes a successful evaluation of what is known and not known at the outset' (1989:91). Again our two corpora from Round I and II differ significantly from one another in this respect.

The more advanced learner corpus of Round II contains many instances in which students manage to first explore common ground and thus establish a communicative basis before elaborating the topic. It is structures like 'I have heard that you', 'you remember…', keywords like 'together', and certain tag questions which achieve this goal, as in the following exchange:

(4)
a   So, *I have heard* you have a horse.
b   The, the place that we stayed *together*, in that cabin. (five occurrences)
c   I think, eh, you are going to Thailand, *aren't you*? (four occurrences)
d   Do you *remember* when we have the children from Poland here?
     (seven occurrences)

These items and structures had not yet emerged in the Round I talks – apart from two tag questions. The more learners manage to refer to and incorporate shared knowledge, the more the interactions move away from a didactically motivated activity and approach naturally occurring conversations between peers.

Gambits as markers of discourse authenticity
Gambits as defined by Edmondson and House (1981) refer to those items in spoken discourse which do not – like interactional moves – forward the conversation, but are mainly used as 'discourse lubricants' that might serve a variety of different interactional functions. They allow speakers, for example, to gain time and thus keep up the smooth flow of conversation. They play a crucial role in turn-taking, and, as back-channel responses, they signal speakers that their partner attends to the message.

Gambits are explicitly taught neither in the traditional nor in an autonomous classroom, and classroom English is normally characterised by their under-representation (cf. Edmondson and House, 1981:69ff). They tend to emerge only when language learners have become conversationally more proficient, and have developed an ear for authentic, naturally-occurring conversations between native speakers. Any increase in types and tokens of gambits between the two data collection stages would thus point to an advancement in the conversational development of the learners under discussion, and could thus perhaps be interpreted as a movement towards more native-speaker-like behaviour.

A closer look at the overall frequencies and distributions of gambits in the two corpora reveals a highly differentiated picture (Table 4).

Table 4 Gambit types and tokens

Gambit type	Round I			Round II	
	n	Tokens		n	Tokens
Receipts	149	yes (72); yeah (36); mhm (27); ok (9); ah(a) (4); I see (1)		167	yeah (67); yes (65); ok (20); repetition (11); mhm (4)
Go-ons	19	yes? (13); repetition (2); yeah? (1); aha? (1); oh? (1); mhm? (1)		11	yeah? (5); yes? (4); oh? (2)
Starters	19	so (8); oh (4); well (2); yeah (1); but (1); now (1); yes (1)		36	well (11); so (11); but (8); ok (3); yeah (2); oh (1)
Exclaims	10	oh! (7); ah! (2); oh, yes! (1)		26	oh! (11); oh, yeah! (8); great! (3); that's nice! (1); oh, wow! (1); oh, my God! (1); you lucky bastard! (1)
Cajolers	0	–		16	you know (11); I mean (5); you know what I mean (1)
Appealers	2	tag questions (2)		9	tag questions (6); remember? (2); ok? (1)

Whereas Uptaker subtypes like Receipts and Go-ons are already well-represented after 17 months of English, Cajolers like 'I know', 'I mean', which are often intended to make a message more 'palatable' to the hearer, seem to be indicative of a later developmental stage. The same holds true of Starters like 'well'. The following excerpt (5) from the Round II talks might serve as an illustration. The learners talk about student AN's visit to a rock festival:

(5)
A: I'm going to miss you.
AN: *Well*, it's only four days, and I am going home at night. I'm not allowed to be out there at night, 'cause my mom is (1 sec)
A: (unintelligible)
AN: Yeah, she is. She is, *you know*, very careful (1 sec) (?).
A: That's moms.
AN: Yeah.
A: So, *well*, what about your dad?

(Round II talks)

Cajolers cannot be observed in Round I talks, and Starter 'well' occurs only twice. By contrast, Appealers, which are often realised as tag questions, are used in neither corpus in greater numbers. Whether this goes to show that Appealers have not yet been internalised as interactional devices to the same extent as other gambit types, or whether this is due to situational factors (i.e. peers talking about 'safe topics'), cannot be decided on the basis of these data alone. The same holds true for Underscorers. Tokens that explicitly draw the hearer's attention to part of the message and highlight it – like 'the point is', 'listen', 'look' etc. – are completely absent from both rounds of talk.

In sum, the overall frequencies of Uptakers (i.e. Receipts and Go-ons) did not change significantly between the two rounds of talks (Round I: n=168 vs. Round II: n=178). However, the number of gambit tokens other than Uptakers almost tripled within the time-span of two and a half years (n=31 vs. n=88).

'Charged input': trouble management and negotiation for meaning

Since Hatch (1978) stressed the importance of verbal interactions for the linguistic development of foreign language learners, SLA researchers have tried to identify discourse features which are likely to play a crucial role in language learning, i.e. discourse features which facilitate verbal processing and cause the linguistic structures to emerge and grow in learners. It is especially inter-actional devices for overcoming comprehension problems and when negotiating meaning that seem to support the acquisitional process. The list of conversational strategies and linguistic means mentioned in this context includes: self- and other-corrections, collaborative sentence completions, prompts, clarification requests, comprehension checks, confirmation checks, repetitions etc. (e.g. Long, 1981, 1983; Porter, 1986).

The line of argument which the so-called 'Interaction Hypothesis' rests upon is an indirect one: Whatever promotes comprehension also facilitates acquisition, since comprehensible input must be regarded as a prerequisite for learning. Although many critics have pointed out that the relationship between comprehensible input and acquisition is far from clear (Faerch and Kasper, 1986; Wagner, 1996 etc.), it can be assumed that communicative trouble 'charges' (Stevick, 1980) the input, so that deep-processing is more likely to occur.

However, it is not only the repair of communicative trouble that is particularly well-suited to trigger and promote learning. Metalinguistic reflections and/or discussions of any kind will focus the learners' attention on the forms of language and thus support the learning process. Focal attention on formal features allows learners to notice discrepancies between their interlanguage and target language structures, which is claimed to be a conditioning factor for developmental progress. This latter issue has also been raised by Swain (1985, 1997) who stressed that 'pushed output', in which the learners have to stretch their linguistic resources, also leads to attendance to form. Whenever learners are forced to make their contributions more precise, coherent and appropriate, learning can – as it were – be witnessed 'in progress' (Swain and Lapkin, 1998).

In short, it is plausible to assume that whatever facilitates comprehension and triggers 'gap noticing' helps to 'charge' the input and thus promotes learning in more or less (in-)direct ways. However, the notion of 'charged input' needs to be interpreted in even more general terms. Social psychologists and discourse analysts have pointed out again and again that any conversational interaction involves negotiation at various levels. When negotiating meaning and conversational outcomes interlocutors are at the same time – and by implication – engaged in face-work, i.e. they try to enhance their self-image and project a favourable image of themselves. When they are thus involved as whole persons working to reassert their identity and negotiate their role in the interaction, the input (and output) gets 'charged' and is deep-processed.

And it is also negotiation in this wider sense of the word that tends to make learner-learner interactions valuable from an acquisitional point of view. The input is 'charged' whenever the interaction is interpreted as a socially and psychologically relevant event by the speakers, i.e. when learners are engaged in face-work, express their genuinely felt desires and beliefs, work hard to reach conversational outcomes and thus collaboratively construct a meaningful discourse.

The crucial issue in the EFL context is whether and to what extent these features also characterise learner-learner interactions as they are allowed to develop in institutionalised settings. Several observational classroom studies have come to the conclusion that ' "negotiating for meaning" is not a strategy that language learners are predisposed to employ when they encounter gaps in their understanding.' (Foster, 1998:1) The frequency of these events is largely determined by the participants' perceptions of the problems of the interaction and their views on the 'fatality' of the consequences of non- or half-understanding. In traditional classrooms learners all too often resort to a face-saving 'feigning strategy', thus conveying the impression of a trouble-free interaction (cf. also Aston, 1986).

A closer look at peer-to-peer talks in the autonomous classroom, however, yields a slightly more differentiated picture. It is here that the overall educational goal of 'taking charge of one's own learning' seems to counteract the frequently observed 'typical' learner behaviour. To the extent that learners have managed to take over responsibility for their own learning, they are also prepared and willing to engage in meaningful discourse construction including repair management, the quality of which is also determined by the developmental stage and thus the level of communicative proficiency. The two rounds of peer-to-peer talks do not seem to differ significantly as regards the frequency of interactional modifications mentioned above, but rather as regards the sophistication and complexity of their verbal realisations. The excerpts in the following two sections will illustrate the point.

Trouble management and pushed output:
evidence from weak learners in Round I talks

It comes as a surprise that it is not only the better students in the Round I talks whose interactions contain many instances of trouble-shooting and repair management. The following excerpts (6 to 10) all involve probably the three weakest learners in the class when it comes to linguistic accuracy. It is especially learner D who – despite his limited linguistic resources – displays a remarkable ability to keep the conversation going and to push his partners into more comprehensible output.[6]

(6)
D: Ehm, what should you do in Poland?
LO: Everything.
D: What? (3 sec)
LO: Buy something (.) present for my mum and dad
...
LO: Yes. (2.5 sec) Out that (?). (5 sec)
D: What?
LO: Who should you stand with in Poland?
D: What?
LO: Who should you live with in Poland?
D: Ehm, a boy named Martin.

(Round I talks)

Compare also the next example in (7), in which learner D acts similarly to a native speaker in foreigner talk discourse. He starts out with an open wh-question, and on not succeeding in drawing learner LO into the conversation, desperately tries to prevent the communication from breaking down, and finally asks a *yes/no*-question, which allows LO to respond in a very brief but meaningful way. Long's foreigner talk discourse data also contain evidence that native speakers tend to replace *wh*-questions by *yes/no*-questions when the communication is about to run into trouble.

(7)
D: What should you do tomorrow?
LO: I don't know.
D: Try to think of something.
LO: Uh, I cannot think about this. Uh.
D: Should you up and ride your horse?
LO: No.

(Round I talks)

Learner D's two peer-to-peer talks abound with repair work and hearer-supportive moves. He takes over responsibility for the success of the interaction similarly to native speakers in foreigner talk discourse. The following excerpts contain illustrations of a confirmation check as in (8), sentence sharing and other-repair – in (9) and (10) respectively.

(8)
D: What did, what's should you do today?
L: Today I ehm, I shall have my birthday.
D: Have you birthday today?
L: Yes.
D: Happy birthday.
L: Thank you, so I should home and, and make made a cake to my-
D: birthday cake?

L: Cake, yes…

(Round I talks)

(9)
L: …(2 sec) I get ehm phh, get up in my bed and (?) to eat my (.)
D: breakfast
L: Yes, breakfast, and…

(Round I talks)

(10)
D: What did you?
LO: I going to read my horse? (1 sec)
D: Ride.
LO: Riding.

(Round I talks)

Many researchers and language practitioners have argued that a classroom which relies too heavily on pair and group work might not provide sufficient and adequate stimuli for the linguistic – and especially the sociolinguistic – development of learners. They claim that language input from peers is too deficient in quantity and quality. Porter states, for example: 'The underlying issue is whether the learners can learn various features of sociolinguistic competence from each other. The findings suggest that they cannot' (1986: 215).

The obvious question is, of course, what is understood by 'sociolinguistic competence'? If it implies the learners' ability to:

- show empathy and interest in what the partner is saying
- regularly provide feedback cues and signal 'active listening'
- provide linguistic support in case of communicative trouble
- plug conversational gaps
- uphold principles of politeness

and so on, then the examples from the weaker learners cited above provide counter-evidence. They might, however, be used to support the argument of the paucity of learner language in formal terms, and underline the misgiving that too much deviant learner input in group work will possibly lead to a stable pidginised form of learner language (cf. Pica and Doughty, 1985; Aston, 1986).

One result of the LAALE project is, however, that the grammatical development up to the fourth year of English, i.e. the time of the Round II talks, did not come to a standstill. On the contrary, a comparison with traditionally-taught learners showed that the autonomous learners' grammatical proficiency compared extremely well with that of learners who had been systematically subjected to formal instruction (cf. Legenhausen, 1999a).

Negotiation for meaning: Round II talks

In the Round II talks, i.e. after four years of learning English, there are a host of examples of elaborate sequences in which learners struggle hard – and over many turns – to come to an agreement on the meaning of concepts and terms. The following discussion (11) revolves around the connotations of the term 'relationship'.

(11)
N:　　Have you wri-, only written one letter to him [pen friend] and that he
　　　not-
MA:　He did not answer the letter (1 sec) so I think that it was (2.5 sec)
N:.　　　　　　　　　　　　　　　　okay yeah　　　　　　　　　the end of
　　　your relationship
MA:　Relationship?
N:　　Relationship, friendship.
MA:　Yes.
N:　　Friendship, okay.
MA:　I'm not a gay.
N:　　No (1 sec) okay [laughing]. I, I still have contact with my friend
　　　Anieska.

(Round II talks)

In excerpt (12) the students talk about the new school which learner M is going to attend. Although LA seems to have some general knowledge of the type of school, he is not at all clear what this implies. They are making a cooperative effort to work it out together.

(12)
LA:　What are you going to do in your new school, isn't it a special school?
M:　　No, it's just a (.)
LA:　　　　　　　　　an ordinary school
M:　　No, it's a after school?
LA:　After school? I don't know what it's called in English.
M:　　It's (.) I think it's a kind of private school maybe.
LA:　Are you going to live there?
M:　　Yeah, go (.) only going home in the (.)
LA:　　　　　　　　　　　　　　weekends?
M:　　Yeah, every second holiday of the weekend. I don't know.

(Round II talks)

Similar discussions about concepts lacking in the target language like 'After Skole' in (12) or about the connotational range of certain terms such as 'relationship' in (11) might as well have occurred between native speakers. They can only be observed in Round II talks, and are indicative of the high level of sociopragmatic competence of the learners involved.

Conclusion

The data clearly show that the concern expressed in the literature that learner languages as they develop in institutional settings cannot reach higher levels of sociolinguistic or sociopragmatic sophistication, whether true for traditional classrooms or not, does not apply to autonomous classrooms of the type under discussion. The same holds true for the misgiving that classrooms which set great store by group work and refrain from explicit formal instruction might lead to early fossilisation. The LAALE data provide ample evidence that this is not the case in the setting investigated, i.e. if principles of autonomous language learning are implemented.

It has been shown elsewhere that the communicative behaviour of the learners under discussion contrasts markedly with learners who follow a traditional textbook-based syllabus (cf. Legenhausen, 1999b). The class of traditional learners who were subjected to the same data elicitation procedures approached the task of talking to one another about a topic of their own choice with, as it were, a 'didactic' attitude. The majority of them avoided risk-taking by sticking to safe textbook phrases which they had memorised. Only rarely did discourse features of the type outlined above emerge.

The difference in behaviour can be seen as the direct result of the methodological principles implemented in the classrooms. The autonomous classroom is characterised by the authenticity of social and communicative interactions, and by the importance it attributes to awareness-raising as regards communication as a process; language as a system, and the learning process itself (cf. Dam, 1995). These principles combine and work together to allow learners to develop their communicative competence. ▓

Notes

1 Dam started the *Experiment in Beginning English* in Denmark in 1975. Cf. also the classroom implementations of the Freinet pedagogy in France and elsewhere.
2 Transcription conventions:
(.) indicates a pause shorter than a second.
(?) unintelligible word or phrase.
3 The difference between Round I and Round II talks is statistically highly significant at the p<0.0005 level (t-test for independent means: t = 6.02: df = 132). I owe the statistics to N. Bretschneider, unpublished Staatsexamensarbeit.
4 According to the Chi-square test, the difference between the two rounds of talks is highly significant at the p<0.0001 level ($x2$ = 20.79; df = 1).
5 The difference is significant at the p<0.0001 level ($x2$ = 86.78).
6 Students D, LO, and L are the only learners in the group who at this stage still have retained deviant 'should' (instead of 'will'), which is an interference error caused by their Danish mother tongue.

References

Aston, G. (1986) Trouble-shooting in interaction with learners: the more the merrier? *Applied Linguistics*, 7:128-43.
Cook, G. (1989) *Discourse*. Oxford: Oxford University Press.
Dam, L. (1995) *Learner Autonomy 3: from theory to classroom practice*. Dublin: Authentik.
Dam, L. and Legenhausen, L. (1996) The acquisition of vocabulary in an autonomous learning environment – the first months of beginning English. In R. Pemberton et al. (eds) *Taking Control: autonomy in language learning*. Hong Kong: Hong Kong University Press.
Edmondson, W. and House, J. (1984) *Let's Talk and Talk about it: a pedagogic interactional grammar of English*. München: Urban and Schwarzenberg.
Faerch, K. and Kasper, G. (1986) The role of comprehension in second language acquisition. *Applied Linguistics*, 7:198-217.
Foster, P. (1998) A classroom perspective on the negotiation of meaning. *Applied Linguistics*, 19:1-23.
Hatch, E. (1978) Discourse analysis and second language acquisition. In E. Hatch (ed.) *Second Language Acquisition: a book of readings*. Rowley, Mass.: Newbury House.
Legenhausen, L. (1999a) Language acquisition without grammar instruction? The evidence from an autonomous classroom. *Revista Canaria de Estudios Ingleses*, 38:63-76.
Legenhausen, L. (1999b) Traditional and autonomous learners compared. The impact of classroom culture on communicative attitudes and behaviour. In Ch. Edelhoff and R. Weskamp. (eds) *Autonomes Sprachenlernen*. München: Hueber.
Long, M. (1981) Questions in foreigner talk discourse. *Language Learning*, 31:135-57.
Long, M. (1983) Native speaker / non-native speaker conversation and the negotiation of comprehensible input. *Applied Linguistics* 4:126-41.
Pica, T. and Doughty, C. (1985) The role of group work in classroom second language acquisition. *Studies in Second Language Acquisition*, 7:233-48.
Porter, P. (1986) How learners talk to each other: input and interaction in task-centred discussions. In Day, R.R. (ed.) *Talking to Learn: conversation in second language acquisition*. Rowley, Mass.: Newbury House.
Stevick, E. (1980) *Teaching Languages: a way and ways*. Rowley, Mass.: Newbury House.
Swain, M. (1985) Communicative competence: some roles of comprehensible input and comprehensible output in its development. In S. Gass and C. Madden (eds) *Input in Second Language Acquisition*. Rowley, Mass etc.: Newbury House.
Swain, M. (1997) Collaborative dialogue: its contribution to second language learning. *Revista Canaria de Estudios Ingleses*, 34:115-32.
Swain, M. and Lapkin, S. (1998) Interaction and second language learning: two adolescent French immersion students working together. *Modern Language Journal*, 82:320-37.
Wagner, J. (1996) Foreign language acquisition through interaction: a critical review of research on conversational adjustments. *Journal of Pragmatics*, 26:215-35.

◆ Group work for autonomy in Asia: insights from teacher-research

◆ Le travail de groupe en vue de l'autonomie éclairé par la recherche de l'enseignant: exemples en Asie

Richard C. Smith

University of Foreign Studies, Tokyo, Japan

Abstract

This paper contributes to an ongoing debate regarding the validity of learner autonomy in Asian settings. On both sides of this debate, emphasis has been placed on the particular salience in such settings of interdependence in counterbalance to a perceived over-emphasis on individualism in western conceptions of learner autonomy. Relatively few suggestions have been made for the development of appropriate classroom practice, but a consensus seems to have been emerging that group-based approaches (for example, to self-access) are more likely to be appropriate in Asian contexts than completely individualised learning. In this paper, I present evidence which appears to confirm the feasibility and appropriateness of self-directed group work arrangements in a particular Japanese classroom setting. However, I also attempt to move the debate on by showing how – in the light of practice – the interpretation of autonomy in Asian contexts may need to be further problematised. By means of successive reinterpretations of the classroom data presented, I attempt to counter implications that a group-based approach in itself represents a particularly appropriate 'Asian alternative'. I conclude that further insights from self-critical teacher-research are needed before generalisations can be made with confidence about the nature of appropriate pedagogy for autonomy in this or other Asian settings.

Résumé

Dans le débat actuel sur la validité de la notion d'autonomie de l'apprenant en Asie, il a été souvent souligné que, dans le contexte asiatique, une place importante doit être accordée à la notion d'interdépendance, tandis qu'au contraire les conceptions occidentales de l'autonomie mettent fortement l'accent sur l'individualisme. Les propositions concrètes pour des pratiques de classe appropriées sont encore relativement peu nombreuses, mais un consensus semble s'être établi sur l'idée que les approches préconisant un travail en groupes (par exemple pour l'usage des centres de ressources) seraient plus efficaces en contexte asiatique que celles préconisant un apprentissage purement individuel. Dans cet article, je présente une description de ma pratique dans une université japonaise qui semble confirmer que le travail en groupes auto-dirigés est possible et efficace dans ce contexte. Cependant, j'essaie aussi de contribuer à la définition d'une nouvelle perspective en montrant – à la lumière de la pratique – combien il resterait encore à problématiser plus finement l'interprétation de l'autonomie dans les contextes asiatiques.

Autonomy in Asia: how can it be appropriate?

Theoretical justifications At the 1996 AILA Conference, Aoki Naoko and I presented several counter-objections to suggestions made by, among others, Jones (1995) that a 'retreat from autonomy' is called for in Asia. Drawing attention to prevalent misconceptions regarding the nature both of 'autonomy' and of 'culture', we proposed that learner autonomy, defined with full regard to requirements for interdependence as well as independence, can be seen as a valid goal in Japanese settings (Aoki and Smith, 1996). At the same conference, Little (1996) added further weight to this position, reemphasising that,

> Because we are social beings our independence is always balanced by dependence; our essential condition is one of interdependence.

and, more positively:

> Our capacity for self-instruction probably develops out of our experience of learning in interaction with others: in order to teach ourselves, we must create an internal substitute for ... interaction. (Little, 1991:5)

The suggestion that attempts to enhance learner autonomy in Asia do not necessarily involve an imposition of western individualist values received further theoretical support at the November 1996 Autonomy 2000 conference in Thailand. In particular, two Hong Kong-based presenters, Benson and Littlewood, reemphasised (in separate papers) that autonomy need not be conceived of as excluding values such as collaboration and interdependence which are frequently associated with Asian cultures, and that social definitions of autonomy may be particularly salient in Asian contexts (Benson, 1996; Littlewood, 1996).

Taken together, these theoretical clarifications seem to provide some support for continuing, culturally sensitive pedagogical experimentation involving the idea of learner autonomy in Asian contexts (Smith, 1997), and it is to the relatively under-considered issue of appropriate methodology that I shall devote most attention in this paper.

Suggestions for appropriate methodology Means for enhancing learner autonomy are likely to have to vary to fulfil the different requirements of appropriateness in different cultural contexts (Aoki and Smith, 1996). Here, then, are some of the suggestions for appropriate methodology in Asia which have been made to date:

> Hong Kong appears to be a group-oriented society; consequently, the [learner training for self-access] programmes are as far as possible group driven and group negotiated. (Farmer, 1994:16)

> One feature of [Cambodian students'] learning style, a tendency to work (and enjoy working) collaboratively, may be seized upon as inspiration for ideas in culturally-friendly self-access. (Jones, 1995:230)

> The power of ingroup cohesion on [class] members' motivation … cannot be underestimated. Such motivation impels participants to …make autonomous decisions and act upon them with a force and conviction that would not be conceivable in an ordinary classroom. (Ho and Crookall, 1995:242)

As is clear from these quotations, both Farmer (1994) and Jones (1995) make claims – on the basis of generalisations relating to Hong Kong Chinese and Cambodian learners, respectively – about the local appropriateness of group- as opposed to individual-centred approaches to the use of self-access centres, while Ho and Crookall (1995) suggest – on the basis of their own analysis of Chinese learner characteristics – that a classroom-based simulation approach in Hong Kong succeeded largely because students worked towards achievement of collective goals, as members of a team.

Whereas these suggestions are framed rhetorically as seeming to imply, respectively, 'limits on independence' (Farmer, 1994), a 'retreat' from autonomy (Jones, 1995) and a possible 'break' with local traditions (Ho and Crookall, 1995), they can be reinterpreted – in the light of the theoretical clarifications reviewed above – as attempts to engage in appropriate pedagogy for learner autonomy which take into account perceived learner requirements for interdependence in Cambodia and Hong Kong. The practical emphasis of these authors on group work seems to be fully consistent not only with theoretical emphases on the social nature of learner autonomy but also with further reports on practice in Japanese university settings which seem to imply that collaborative arrangements are appropriate (Aoki and Smith, 1996; Smith, 1996; Robbins, 1996).

Thus, practical suggestions to date have most frequently been justified with reference either to explicit generalisations about different Asian nationalities' 'group-orientedness' (Farmer, 1994; Ho and Crookall, 1995; Jones, 1995; Robbins, 1996), or to theoretical emphases on the particular salience in Asian contexts of 'interdependence', emphases which seem themselves to be based on an assumption that Asian learners are relatively group-oriented.

A consensus has begun to emerge that interdependence and group work represent appropriate alternative values which can inform the development of approaches to learner autonomy in Asia. However, it now seems timely to look behind what seem to be the 'alternative stereotypes' (regarding learners' group-orientedness, interdependence and preference for cooperative activity) which have hitherto been relied upon to support suggestions for appropriate methodology in Asian contexts.

What may be most called for at this point in the 'autonomy in Asia' debate are reports of practice which offer new insights not tied to *a priori* generalisations (Smith, 1997). Below, then, I attempt to provide one such report, in the first instance to show how self-directed learning arrangements can be implemented with – apparently – some success in an Asian classroom setting (the few reports of practice to date have mostly focused on self-access and/or learner 'training' rather than classroom-based self-direction), but also as a basis for problematising the notion that group work in itself represents a particularly appropriate 'Asian alternative'.

Self-directed classroom group work in a Japanese university setting

Background Students at the Japanese university focused on here major in a variety of foreign languages and seem to be generally well-motivated to improve their English abilities in comparison with students in many other Japanese university settings (see Umino, 1999, for further detail relating to this institution). The series of lessons I shall describe below occurred in 1994 during the first half of my fourth year as a full-time teacher at the university (this was my ninth year in Japan). The lessons involved 39 first-year students taking an 'English listening' course for students majoring in languages other than English.

This is one of two compulsory English courses non-majors take in their first year, the other (taught by another teacher) being intended to develop reading abilities. Classes meet for one and a half hours per week, over a total of about 28 weeks (about 14 weeks in each of Semesters 1 and 2).

Students' self-directed learning outside class For homework after one of the first lessons, I asked students to reflect in writing on activities they currently engaged in for self-improvement of English listening abilities. Almost all students reported doing something, and their answers to the question 'What – if anything – do you do outside class to improve your listening abilities?' are collated below:

- Do practice listening tests for TOEFL; TOEIC; 'Eiken' exams.
- Listen to ELT audio-tapes (turning down the volume to take the part of one of the speakers).
- Listen to ELT programmes on the radio (repeating aloud; writing down what they say).
- Watch ELT programmes on TV.
- Listen to English songs (reading and studying the lyrics; singing along);
- Listen to English medium radio.
- Watch English language movies on video (trying to ignore subtitles; noting down new words; writing comments; repeating 'cool

expressions'; comparing subtitles with what they actually say; looking at a published screenplay).

- Watch English TV news programmes, documentaries, dramas (noting down new words).
- Overseas phone calls to my friends.
- Joint activities with international students (speaking in English).
- Use English in my part-time job (tour guide; waiter, waitress; babysitter; interpreter).
- Talk in English with my (Japanese) friend.
- Go the movie theatre every Saturday and watch the same (English language) movie repeatedly, trying to ignore the subtitles.

Perhaps it is not entirely surprising that so many of these students were used to working on their English independently, given the intensive self-study many of them had recently engaged in to prepare for university entrance examinations. What did surprise me, however, was the variety of resources employed and the creativity of the tasks which some students had developed for themselves. I found (and reemphasise here) that the majority of these students were far from being other-directed or 'passive' in relation to outside-class learning (Beebe, 1996, and Usuki, 1999, have offered similar observations relating to Japanese students in other settings). This discovery led me to wonder whether self-directed learning arrangements could be implemented inside the classroom.

Following the above homework, I encouraged students to share information regarding the resources and activities they were currently using outside class. Discussion in pairs and small groups was followed by further reflective writing in which I asked students to clarify their goals and plans for the coming year's outside-class learning. In the following lesson, students shared these plans and advised one another with regard to possible improvement. It was clear by this stage that class members had various goals and preferences for improving their English listening abilities and my next step was to ask students to write down ideas for types of resource and activity they would like to engage with in class.

The shift to classroom self-directed learning arrangements then occurred, in the following manner: as students were writing, I went around eliciting their ideas, then summarised these in the form of a menu of possible choices on the board. I then asked students to individually select the resource-type they were most interested in working with in class and I formed groups according to first choices. I then encouraged groups to come up with action plans for the following week's lesson.

Subsequent class sessions throughout the first semester were to be taken up entirely with group work, and it was not until the final lesson of the semester that I asked students to come together again as a whole class.

Group activities as described by students Below I present details of resources used and activities engaged in during this semester by all groups, as far as possible in students' own words (transcribed from video-taped end-of-semester oral reports to the whole class). My additional clarifications are in square brackets.

1) Movies on video (11 students, divided by me into two groups of 5 and 6

students each. This is from the final report of one of the two movie groups):

We watched several kinds of movie …Before we watch the movie, we discuss what the story is about. While we are watching …we sometimes stop the movie when someone can't understand, and others help the person to understand the story well. [By doing] that, each of us can understand the story. After we watch the movie we talk about what scene we like best and why we like the scene.

During this class we found how easy it is to watch movies with English captions. …We also found that watching movies is really helpful for us to improve our English ability very well with lots of fun. We enjoy watching movies every time.

2) TV news or documentaries (9 students):

We watched several short documentaries on video tapes we borrowed from our teacher [from the *Focus on* … series published by ABC/Prentice-Hall, with supporting text materials] …We could use textbooks, so it was not so hard to understand the contents of the news. What we did …was watching a piece of news and solving the problems in the textbook. Sometimes we discussed the contents in Japanese… When the textbook was not in our hands [i.e. when students used programmes they had recorded off-air], we concentrated our numbers [i.e. put our heads together?] and tried to catch the content roughly… As a whole, it was of great interest.

3) TV drama (6 students):

We watch *Full House* [an American sit-com, recorded weekly off-air by one of the students]. At first we watch it in English twice. Then, we try to make clear the part we couldn't understand. After we understand the story, we discuss the differences between American and Japanese conceptions.

4) Songs (6 students):

We …listened to several songs. We each prepared the papers of the words of the song, with some of the words missing. First, we listened to the song once and tried to get the missing words. Then we listened to the song again until we got all of the words. We talked about the answers together, looking at the rhymes and the context… These lessons were not a forced work, so things got a bit sloppy in the end, but I think we could study more freely and happily this way… It was good to have a discussion with the others, in order to have another point of view on guessing the missing words.

5) Conversation (4 students):

We used *Headway* [published by Oxford University Press] for our textbook. Every week, a different coordinator chose a few topics to talk about. Firstly, we used a cassette tape to listen to the topic. Secondly, the coordinator asked us some questions and we answered them. Thirdly, we checked the answers if they are correct or not and talked more about the topic.

6) Lectures (3 students):

At first we chose the textbook. The title was *Study Listening* [published by Cambridge University Press].

As we listened, we answered the questions in the textbook. We also had an answer book, so even if we can't understand well it helped us to improve our ability.

Student evaluations of learning arrangements Prior to the final session of the semester, I asked all students to write individual, open-ended evaluations of within-class arrangements. The positive evaluative comments received are summarised below (categorisation is author's own):

Learning process
    can work at our own pace;
    can enjoy, learn delightedly, have fun; can learn deeply, practically;
    freedom of choice, learning according to own preference; different
    learners have different preferences, so suitable, can follow own interests;
    can attend class actively and positively (because we do what we want);
    interesting, exciting, flexible way of teaching.

Learning products
    improved listening ability;
    learned new strategies and/or resources.

Efficiency
    effective use of limited time;
    can say our opinion many times, more chance to talk to each other,
    can discuss more freely because of small group size.

Social
    can cooperate, help each other understand;
    can make friends.

Responsibility
    we can feel responsible for our own work;
    can work or not work according to own will.

Critical comments included in end-of-semester reports were as follows (categorisation is author's own):

Learning process

too many groups – not enough time to talk with teacher, nobody to ask for advice when problems occur;

we choose what's funny or easy to work with more than what's good for our improvement;

we don't know how to listen actively (i.e. tasks, strategies) – need instruction in this, not sure of own ways for actively using resources, no tasks to do;

not every group has a leader with good command of English – so, can be dull;

logistical problems (e.g. different groups in the same classroom disturb each other with noise);

own lack of active participation;

other group members don't attend regularly, not enough materials as a result.

Learning products

may not have actually improved listening ability, don't know whether improved or not (no measure of this);

only enjoyed, didn't learn;

not enough time to speak English (because of listening focus).

Suggestions for improvement

want more time for English conversation;

should be able to change groups more frequently (can only learn so much from one type of resource, or one group of people).

Subsequent developments At the end of the final session in the semester, I asked students to write notes in answer to the question, 'What do you want to do in class next semester?'. As students wrote, I went around asking individual students the same question. Out of 38 students present, 36 expressed a clear preference for continuation of group work as opposed to whole class arrangements, despite the critical comments indicated above.

These critical comments formed the basis for negotiation of improvements to overall classroom arrangements in the following semester, with the final comments above, for example, having led directly to a more relaxed approach on my part towards prescription of a 'listening' focus and to a revised arrangement involving two 'cycles' of self-directed group learning.

In subsequent years I have continued to pursue and further adapt the above type of approach in other English courses in the same university, attempting to offer regular opportunities for rejection or modification. So far, consistently large majorities of students in all of these courses have voted to continue with and improve on self-directed learning rather than 'revert' to more conventional arrangements.

Complexifying matters:
appropriate interpretation of classroom practice

Above I have presented some classroom data partly in order to show that Japanese students in this university context can display at least partial autonomy, both outside and inside class, to a degree which might appear to contradict prevalent western conceptions regarding (East) Asian learners. More specifically, however, I wish to use this retrospective report as a basis for a critique (partially, at least, a self-critique) with regard to the appropriate interpretation of practice. Although I have previously 'advertised' the approach described above in terms relating to its group-based nature, (Aoki and Smith, 1996; Smith, 1996) a number of qualifications have arisen in my mind as a result of subsequent practice and reflection on practice, which I shall express in the form of a series of questions below:

1) *If generalisations about Asian learners are inadequate as a basis for appropriate methodology, what should be the starting-point?* My decision to experiment with self-directed learning in this classroom context was based on observations which appeared to contradict stereotypes of Japanese learners I had previously to some extent shared (hence my 'surprise', reported above, at the extent to which they engaged in voluntary language learning outside class). It would not, then, be appropriate for me to suggest that the particular observations I made (and the approach I adopted on their basis) are generalisable to other Asian or even Japanese settings; indeed, I would prefer to emphasise that these students and this particular context may be exceptional in many ways. In the light of my own experience, however, I can conclude that teachers need to investigate and define the particularities of their own students rather than accept that stereotypes or other generalisations represent a valid basis for the development or justification of appropriate methodology in an Asian context.

2) *Can we even generalise that group-based arrangements are appropriate for all learners in a particular setting?* I can see now that in my first semester of experimentation I did not follow my own advice (regarding the need for teachers to base appropriate methodology on investigation of their own students) in at least one important respect, concerned namely with my prescription of group work in the classroom. I note now that the majority of outside-class learning activities reported by students involved individual, not cooperative study arrangements, and that this alone seems to falsify the assumption that Japanese students have an overriding preference for cooperative rather than individual learning (Robbins, 1996). My reasons (see below) for engaging students in group work in the classroom did not, then, develop out of the data I had gathered about these learners, although the decision to engage them in self-directed learning did.

In fact, subsequent investigation has shown me that certain students do not take particularly kindly to the group-based aspects of the approach described above, and that they may vote for continuation of the approach for other reasons (see question 4 below). In the light of this subsequent realisation, both the positive and critical evaluations reported by students (above) seem to require careful reconsideration. Students may either enjoy group work for reasons not specifically related to the development of learner autonomy (for example, making friends) or offer criticisms of an over-emphasis on group work for reasons which do relate to this goal (for example, a lack of (teacher-directed) learner training with regard to 'how to listen actively'). Many appear to see group work as an effective means for pursuing their own goals, but others (with more specific goals or with a more 'individual' learning style) may remain unsatisfied.

3) *Might group work be justified for reasons apart from students' 'group-orientedness' or 'requirements for interdependence'?* The majority of students in the class focused on above appeared to respond well to group-based arrangements, but I note now that the reasons they gave involved considerations of efficiency, flexibility and freedom as much as social factors. Thus, one aspect which seems to require further investigation is what group work is associated with and contrasted with in students' minds. Since group work is by no means 'typical' in Japanese high school or university lessons, the overall popularity of group work with these students (and, indeed, self-directed learning itself) may in fact lie in its contrast with normal educational arrangements. The apparent success of group work cannot, then, be related in any simple way to 'traditional group-orientedness' in educational settings. Indeed, it could be related more to the fact that students welcome the chance to give expression to their 'individualistic' side, normally denied in more teacher-centred approaches (Aoki and Smith, 1996).

At the same time, group-based as opposed to individual arrangements may, as much as anything else, be appropriate to the teacher's need for (a sense of) control when self-directed learning is introduced into a relatively large class context. For me, the initial prescription that class work should be carried out in groups which I could easily 'supervise' (and my subsequent (Smith, 1996) interpretations of the success of the experiment in terms relating to its collaborative nature) was – I now realise – a step on the road to 'letting go' further and admitting that individual classroom learning was also feasible and appropriate for some students.

4) *Is the 'group factor' the most salient?* Factors other than their group-based nature may, then, explain the apparent success of the self-directed learning arrangements I have described. What I now feel might be most salient is that control over learning is transferred – in many areas – to students and that they are given the opportunity to modify or reject the overall approach adopted via writing and other one-to-one consultations (Smith, 1998). Re-examination of the evaluations presented above seems to provide some support for this current perception: rather than social advantages, students refer much more to factors such as being able to work at their own pace, having 'freedom of choice', fun, interest, and the development of a sense of responsibility for their own learning, while several of the disadvantages mentioned refer specifically to group dynamics. There may, then, be other variables which made the approach popular but which a focus on the 'group factor' blinded me to at the time.

5) *Might an over-emphasis on the validity of group work disguise inappropriateness in other areas?* Some overall approaches to learner autonomy might have greater

inherent potential for 'cultural incompatibility' in Asian contexts than others – whether or not they engage students in collaborative activity. It might be the case, for example, that the types of 'good language learner' strategy training and/or materials-centred self-access arrangement which are frequently recommended (in both western and Asian contexts) in the name of autonomy tend to involve a greater degree of top-down decision-making, and hence potential for 'inappropriate imposition' than approaches where the enhancement of student control over decision-making (that is, actual self-direction of learning) is made a basic priority.

The approach described above started off, as I have shown, as an attempt to engage in awareness-raising with regard to experiences, goals and ideas students themselves brought to the classroom. On this basis, self-directed learning was then implemented in the classroom with the effect that students were engaged in decision-making in areas they had already demonstrated taking at least partial responsibility for in outside-class learning. The question I end with, then, is: *Are the 'appropriate approaches to autonomy' which have so far been suggested appropriate in respects other than their inclusion of group work; indeed, do they (or indeed my own approach) really constitute valid approaches to the development of (students' own) autonomy in language learning?* Aside from interdependence, 'group-orientedness' and group work, more attention may need to be paid in the future to other values and/or perceptions which might inform the further development of appropriate approaches to autonomy in both Asian and western contexts.

Conclusion

Further, more particular doubts and queries have struck me as I have worked with this type of approach over the last five years, some of which I considered in more detail in my paper at the AILA 1999 conference (Smith, 1999). There I continued to emphasise that arrangements such as those described in the present paper are always 'emergent' (Savage and Storer, 1992), and can never be 'perfectly appropriate', even within a single educational setting.

By focusing in this and my AILA 1999 paper on self-direction in an Asian classroom context and by concentrating on issues concerned with the practical implementation and appropriate interpretation of pedagogy for learner autonomy, I hope that I have succeeded in contributing a fresh perspective to the debate on autonomy in Asia, which has hitherto been carried on at a somewhat abstract, generalised level. Further complexification of the nature of appropriate pedagogy for autonomy in Asian settings is called for in the future, and there is a clear need for continuing, self-critical teacher-research. ▣

References

Aoki, N. and Smith, R.C. (1996) *Autonomy in Cultural Context: the case of Japan.* Paper presented at AILA 1996, Jyväskylä, Finland.

Beebe, J.D. (1996) *Independent Development of English Conversation Skills by Japanese High School Students.* Paper presented at Autonomy 2000, Thonburi, Thailand.

Benson, P. (1996) *The Multiple Meanings of Autonomy in Language Learning.* Paper presented at Autonomy 2000, Thonburi, Thailand.

Farmer, R. (1994) The limits of learner independence in Hong Kong. In D. Gardner and L. Miller (eds) *Directions in Self-Access Language Learning.* Hong Kong: Hong Kong University Press.

Ho, J. and Crookall, D. (1995) Breaking with Chinese cultural traditions: learner autonomy in English language teaching. *System*, 23,2:235-43.

Jones, J. (1995) Self-access and culture: retreating from autonomy. *ELT Journal*, 49,3:228-34.

Little, D. (1991) *Learner Autonomy 1: definitions, issues and problems.* Dublin: Authentik.

Little, D. (1996) *Learner Autonomy is More than a Cultural Construct.* Paper presented at AILA 1996, Jyväskylä, Finland.

Littlewood, W. (1996) *Autonomy in Communication and Learning in the Asian Context.* Paper presented at Autonomy 2000, Thonburi, Thailand.

Robbins, J. (1996) *Language Learning Strategies Instruction in Asia: cooperative autonomy.* Paper presented at Autonomy 2000, Thonburi, Thailand.

Savage, W. and Storer, G. (1992) An emergent language program framework: actively involving learners in needs analysis. *System*, 20,2:187–99.

Smith, R.C. (1996) *Group-centred Autonomous Learning: an 'Asian' contribution?* Paper presented at Autonomy 2000, Thonburi, Thailand.

Smith, R.C. (1997) From Asian views of autonomy to revised views of Asia: beyond autonomy 2000. *Newsletter of the AILA Scientific Commission on Learner Autonomy in Language Learning*, 3:6–9.

Smith, R.C. (1998) *Negotiating Autonomy in a Large Class Context.* Paper presented at JALT 1998, Omiya, Japan.

Smith, R.C. (1999) *Deconstructing 'the Asian Learner': an action research perspective.* Paper presented at AILA 1999, Tokyo, Japan.

Umino, T. (1999) The use of self-instructional broadcast materials for L2 learning: an investigation in the Japanese context. *System*, 27,3:309-27.

Usuki, M. (1999) Promoting learner autonomy: a reconsideration of the stereotypical views about Japanese learners. *Independence*, 24:7–10.

◆ The institutional and psychological context of learner autonomy

◆ Le contexte institutionnel et psychologique de l'autonomie de l'apprenant

Naoko Aoki
Osaka University, Japan

Abstract

This paper is a case study of how institutional and psychological contexts outside the classroom can influence student teachers' attitudes towards autonomy-oriented learning arrangements. It was found that the overall atmosphere or style of the institution, the place and history of the programme in the institution, the place of the teacher in the institution, whether learners feel the programme is their own, learners' goals in being in the class, and tools available to learners to achieve the goals were directly or indirectly reflected in learners' perception of the learning arrangements.

Résumé

Cet article est une étude de cas montrant comment le contexte institutionnel et psychologique à l'extérieur de la classe peut influencer les attitudes d'élèves-professeurs envers des dispositifs éducatifs orientés vers l'autonomie. Il est apparu que l'atmosphère ou le style général de l'institution, la place et l'histoire du programme éducatif au sein de l'institution, la place de l'enseignant dans l'institution, le sentiment d'appropriation du programme par les apprenants, leurs objectifs, et les outils mis à leur disposition pour l'accomplissement de leurs objectifs étaient directement ou indirectement reflétés dans la manière dont les apprenants perçoivent les dispositifs d'apprentissage.

Introduction

The validity of learner autonomy in non–Western cultures has been a great concern to many teachers and researchers (Riley, 1988; Farmer, 1994; Jones, 1995; Ho and Crookall, 1995; Littlewood, 1999). There have also been warnings against attributing problems concerning implementation of autonomous learning to learners' national or ethnic culture too easily (Aoki, 1994; Pierson, 1996; Benson, 1996; Little, 1997; Aoki and Smith, 1999). It is true that certain groups of learners seem to welcome an autonomous mode of learning more than other groups of learners. If culture cannot account for the difference adequately, where should we look for factors determining learners' propensity for autonomy? One area which seems to be worth exploring is the situational context (Benson and Lor, 1998) in which learning takes place. The present paper describes the institutional and psychological context which surrounded the courses I taught, where learner autonomy seemed to be a favourable alternative for student teachers of Japanese as a second language (Aoki, 1996; 1997; 1999), and examines how one student's comments reflected the context.

Contexts

I taught two methodology courses in a Japanese as a Second Language (JSL) teacher-preparation programme at a Japanese university from 1991 to 1997. During that time I gradually developed ways to support and help develop learner autonomy in student teachers. My previous reports on these courses focused on how the students perceived what went on in the classroom (Aoki, 1996; 1997; 1999). After moving to another university, however, I became to suspect that contexts outside the classroom might have provided an optimal environment for my practice. In this section I shall present my reinterpretation of the contexts I was in. It is an ethnographic account of the situation by a complete participant who was known to be a researcher by none including the researcher herself at the time of the observation (Atkinson and Hammersley, 1998), and by no means intended to be an objective description.

The institutional context The setting is a school of education of a middle-ranking national university in Japan. A small undergraduate JSL teacher preparation programme was established in 1989 together with eleven other programmes. The new programmes were full of problems. Only three new teaching positions were allocated to these programmes by the Ministry of

Education. As a result, students in the new programmes had to share most courses with ones in the existing primary and secondary teacher preparation programmes. Although the curricula were interdisciplinary and left quite a lot of room for students' choice, it meant that in practice students had no major field of study. Students complained informally to teachers and formally by writing up a petition to the faculty in 1991. Two questionnaire surveys on students' opinions (Hata et al., 1993; Harada, 1994) showed that the students in the new programmes were significantly less satisfied with the curriculum than those in the primary and secondary teacher preparation programmes. 32.8% of the students in the new programmes had thought of quitting the school, with about 40% of them disappointed with the courses they attended (Hata et al., 1993). The majority of teachers recognised and discussed the problems in both official and unofficial contexts from the beginning, although few significant systematic remedies were found for various reasons until the entire school was restructured in 1998. Both teachers and students shared the view that the new programmes were defective. Whether this shared view was possible because the faculty was conscientious and critical in their orientation or because the problems were too big to ignore may be debatable. Hata et al. (ibid.) admits, however, that it took some courage for the authors to publish the result of the survey. They were honest in writing up the report, and I do not think it would have been possible without support from other faculty members. In that respect I would say the faculty was conscientious and critical.

My position in the context Like many other teachers teaching at Japanese universities, I had quite a high degree of autonomy in terms of the content and the process of the courses I taught. I had to write syllabi, but I did not have to account for my decisions to anyone. It was a tacit agreement among teachers not to criticise each others' teaching. I had few colleagues to discuss issues related with learner autonomy, but I did not feel any pressure to teach in a certain way or another, either. I was able to make moment-by-moment decisions through interaction with my students without worrying about whether my decisions were acceptable to someone other than the students or myself.

   In addition to the general teacher autonomy I enjoyed, I had a privilege arising out of the fact that I was one of the three teachers who were hired for the new programmes. Many staff, both teaching and administrative, seemed to think that my voice should be heard as far as the new programmes, particularly the JSL teacher preparation programme of which I was in charge, were concerned. The discourse that the programmes were defective became a tool for me. I was able to manage otherwise difficult negotiations (e.g. allocation of rooms) successfully because I was speaking for the students in the new programmes. Quite a few influential senior teachers provided moral support (and probably preliminary negotiations behind the scenes too). In retrospect, this nurtured my feeling of self-efficacy (Bandura, 1997) and sense of belonging to the faculty. My position also required active involvement in the administrative work for the JSL teacher-preparation programme, which provided me with opportunities to learn how the system officially worked and how rules could be bent for the students. In other words, I was able to master and appropriate the institutional system in which I worked.

Job prospects for students As was reported in a local newspaper (*Haru ni sakanai puro no yume*, 1993), the job prospects for JSL teaching graduates were not at all rosy. Although nearly one percent of the total population of the country is estimated to be second language speakers, the majority are immigrant workers who cannot attend commercial language courses. Their learning of Japanese is supported by volunteers with little or no financial aid from public funds. The number of JSL teachers who can make a living by teaching is very much limited. Employers tend to prefer mature teachers, leaving little room for university graduates. Schemes to send young teachers overseas looked too competitive for the students I taught. A group of students researched the job prospects for JSL teachers one year. In the reflection on this activity, one student wrote that the more she researched, the more she felt it was impossible to become a JSL teacher.

Psychological context of students The survey conducted by Hata et al. (1993) found that only 31.4% of the first-year students regarded university as a place to acquire either specialist academic knowledge or the knowledge and skills necessary in their future work and that the percentage dropped towards the fourth year. 46.9% regarded a university, rather, as a place for personal development through various experiences, and the figure went up to 60.1% in the fourth year. The same survey also found that whereas nearly 70% of the first year students regarded studying as one of the two most important aspects of student life, the figure dropped to approximately 50% in the second year and remained the same in the third and fourth years. Relationships with friends and club activities come in the second and third respectively. Harada (1994) reported that the students in the new programmes were less satisfied with their relationship with friends on campus. Although what might have caused this result is not discussed in Harada's (ibid.) report, it might be that the students in the new programmes were a minority in the school of education and the general tendency of students to socialise only with in-group members (e.g. same high school, same programme, same club, and so on) made it more difficult for them to develop an extensive network of friends. These figures seem to show that the majority of the students had the will to grow as a person, but that courses offered at the university tended to fail to meet their expectations. Students tried to achieve their goals with other means instead, most notably through relationships with friends, but ones in the new programmes were less successful.

My goals The two courses which I taught was perceived as two parts of a whole both by the students and myself. One of them was compulsory for the students enrolled in the programme. My objective was originally to cover a basic procedure of course design with underlying theories of language use, learning and language learning. I also hoped that I might be able to show the students that learning could be fun as a byproduct of the process of achieving the objective. After I discovered that the students wanted to learn in spite of their seeming reluctance, I transformed the original objective (Aoki, 1996: 253). My new aim was to provide the students with opportunities to reflect on their learning experiences and introduce alternative ways of learning. In other words, as I wrote in answer to a student's question, I wanted to show them that being an autonomous learner feels good.

I had other goals too, however. There were a substantial number of students who were not in the programme because of their interest in JSL. The programme was a second choice for some. Others wanted to study Japanese linguistics or literature. Wherever their real interest lay, I felt I was responsible for the well-being of all students in the programme. I didn't want to exclude anyone from my courses because they had no desire to teach. So I did not include the acquisition of any particular teaching skills in my agenda. I focused on developing an accepting relationship among the teacher and the students because I simply wanted everyone to feel comfortable with being in the class, and because an accepting relationship was thought to support the development of learner autonomy (Rogers, 1980; Nedelsky, 1989; Ryan, 1991).

A case study

In this section, I shall focus on one student who took my courses and show how her comments reflect the contexts described above. This student was chosen for several reasons. First, she was in the last batch of students I taught till their graduation. I was going to interview them, and assumed that their memory would still be fresh. Second, my approach changed over time. The ways I worked with the last batch of students were assumed to best reflect my current way of thinking. Third, this student was among those who most positively responded to the idea of learner autonomy of over one hundred students I worked with in seven years.

Data The data used for the present study consist of the student's writings from the 1996-97 school year and my journal entries and recollections of the same period. The student's writings were an initial contract of participation, reflections at the end of each class and two self-evaluations conducted in the middle of and at the end of the year, which amount to the total of 34 handwritten B5 notebook pages. My journal entries amount to 20 pages, mainly notes of what we did in class with occasional reference to 'memorable incidents' such as a change in the pattern of classroom interaction. In addition, the student was interviewed over the telephone for the purpose of the present paper in the spring 1999, one year after her graduation. The interview was only loosely structured, and explored two major issues (cf. Kvale, 1996 for types of interviews):

- What made her actively participate in the methodology courses?
- How did the perceived reasons relate to the contexts described above?

The interview lasted for approximately 16 minutes and was recorded with the interviewee's permission. Following is a narrative (Connelly and Clandinin, 1990) based on the data. All quotations have been translated from Japanese into English.

Yuki Yuki's mother had very positive experiences at university. She met a variety of people and had a variety of experiences. She often told Yuki about her experiences, and Yuki, too, went to university hoping she would be able to talk with many people of many kinds and with many different ideas. Her purpose was not to study. She did not perceive university as a place for professional training. She would, instead, welcome anything that could be learned. In retrospect, Yuki thinks what she learned at university was subjectivity. Because no one told her what to do, she was in a situation where she was able to choose what she liked and decide to do it for herself. Because those decisions were her own, she was determined to succeed, which was the source of her motivation. She would act on her own and try to solve any problems she encountered. She had always followed other people at high school, but she gradually learned to express her opinions through club activities. People she would share her view with were, however, still rather limited when she started coming to the methodology courses. She did not have any contacts with the other students in the same programme except greeting them when she met them.

In April 1996, when the courses started, Yuki seemed to keep some distance from other students. She did not show any overt interest in JSL, and I was worried if she felt comfortable in the class. Below is her written response to my question, *What, if anything, negatively affected your motivation in this course?*

> In the first Wednesday class we shut down some of our senses like closing eyes and not speaking and felt the lack of information. It was fun, and I was able to actually feel the difficulty of communication due to the lack of information. I thought it was a very good lesson. But at the end of the class we were told that the class wouldn't be over till everyone made comments. I didn't like it at all because I hate giving my opinions in public (although I may look otherwise).

In a few months, however, she seemed to have overcome her resistance. In the mid-year self-evaluation in July, she describes the change in her motivation as:

> As I wrote before I thought I didn't like this course when each of us had to state our opinion, but after that it's been very interesting because each class is different. I'm happy about it. I wasn't late for the class because I didn't want to come. I'd be absent if I didn't.

And to the question, *How do you evaluate yourself and why?* she writes:

> I think I can give myself an A. (It's absolutely an A, compared with other courses.) This is because the initial inertia is completely gone, and I was able to make comments in group discussions and listened to others trying to understand them. But my grade may not be an A because I still find it difficult to speak in a whole class discussion.

Finally what she wanted to learn in the rest of the course was:

> In the second half of the year I want to be able to be active in front of everyone. Then, maybe, I will be able to think in a different way.

Yuki now thinks that the courses were interesting because they were not lectures and she was able to think and act on her own. She did not intend to teach JSL, but the irrelevance of the course content to her future did not bother her at all. In her final self-evaluation, Yuki expresses her satisfaction with her achievement:

> I wasn't comfortable with speaking to the whole class in the beginning, but I tried to speak as much as possible. I think I was able to say all I felt and thought in group discussions. I was able to express my thoughts in this course more than any other courses. And it was fun. I hadn't had much contact with people in the same programme before, and it was really good this course enabled me to make friends with them.

Yuki brought to the last class of the year some cake she baked and coffee in a jar for everyone. The friendship Yuki gained lasted beyond the courses. Yuki says that the students in the JSL teacher preparation programme were said to lack group cohesion in their first and second years, but that they were very close to each other when they graduated. Yuki and the five other female students, some of whom live rather far, had a get-together last summer, and plans another one for this coming summer too.

Asked how she perceived the defective programme, Yuki reacted: 'What? Was it really defective as some suspected?' She thought it was the best programme in the school when she chose to apply. Although she found its shortcomings after she started her study, they did not disappoint her at all. She thinks that the programme had more choices in the curriculum compared with the primary and secondary programmes and allowed her to study a wide range of topics.

Yuki now goes to a vocational school to be a dietician. She wanted to learn more about nutrition, and she feels she is now studying what she wants to. She has been offered a job in a food company starting April 2000, and is planning to take an examination for advanced qualification which requires a minimum of two years' working experience in the field.

Conclusion

In the previous section, I tried to let Yuki's voice tell her story while preserving my voice as a teacher-researcher. In so doing, I found the following direct and indirect connections in the story to the contexts previously described:

> 1 Yuki's purpose for being enrolled in a university programme is not exceptional, but reflects a general tendency among students at the school of education found in Hata et al. (1993). The situation she was in before she took the methodology courses also seem to coincide with the finding by Harada (1994).

> 2 The 'defective curriculum' is perceived by Yuki as something that allowed her choices. This positive interpretation seems to be due to her purpose to be at university.

> 3 Yuki now seems to identify herself with the programme she studied in. In other words, the programme is her own. This may partly explain her positive 'restorying' (Connelly and Clandinin, 1990) of the

programme.

4 The 'defective curriculum' is also thought to have left a lot of room for Yuki to participate in club activities, where she developed her subjectivity. These activities seem to have constituted a significant groundwork for my practice.

5 A tool I utilised to support students' autonomy and to make everyone comfortable in the class, i.e. an accepting relationship among the teacher and the students, matched with Yuki's purpose for being in the university, thus enabling her to use the tool to achieve her goal.

6 The overall atmosphere or style of the institution, the place and history of the programme in the institution, and my position in the institution indirectly influenced Yuki's perception of the courses in that these factors seems to have been influential in determining my goals, thus making her goal achievable.

Connelly and Clandinin (1990:10) claims that 'the empirical narrativist helps his or her reader by self-consciously discussing the selections made, the possible alternative stories, and other limitations seen from the vantage point of "I the critic".' I shall list three such limitations here. First, I could have presented a story told by another student.[1] Another story would have shown a different picture. Second, I followed Yuki's account in selecting the quotations from her writings. Yuki's story could have been told as a history of development of reflective ability and probably as something else too if I had selected other parts of her writings. Third, Yuki's story was told in her relationship with me. Although we developed a trusting relationship when we worked together and I did not detect any change in her attitude at the time of the interview, we are still an ex-teacher and an ex-student, which must have inevitably influenced the content of the story. Her story could be totally different, if told to someone else.

Connelly and Clandinin (1990) present 16 criteria for a good narrative. Among them is invitational quality, and they propose a test of asking readers questions such as, 'What do you make of it for your teaching (or other) situation?' (ibid.:8)

Note

1   I interviewed six students who took both of the two methodology courses and provided a copy of their writings for the purpose of my research. My apologies to Keiko, Shinobu, Tomomi, Yuko, and Yutaka for being unable to include their stories in this paper.

References

Aoki, N. (1994) Autonomy in Asia. *Learning Learning*, ¼,9-12. (Also in *Independence*, 12:4-6.)

Aoki, N. (1996) Mirai no kyooshi no empowerment: gakushuusha to shite no jiritsu o mezashite. In O. Nakajo, (ed.) *Ronshuu Kotoba to Kyooiku*. Kyoto.

Izumi Shoin (1997) Empowering future teachers: A humanistic approach to developing learner autonomy. In G. Gabrielsen (ed.) *Fifth Nordic Conference of Developing Autonomous Learning in the Foreign Language Classroom*. Danmarks Laererhojskole, Copenhagen, August 24-27 1995.

Izumi Shoin (1999) Affect and the role of teachers in the development of learner autonomy. In J. Arnold (ed.) *Affect in Language Learning*. Cambridge: Cambridge University Press.

Aoki, N. and Smith, R. (1999) Learner autonomy in cultural context: the case of Japan. In D. Crabbe and S. Cotterall (eds) *Learner Autonomy in Language Learning: defining the field and effecting change*. Frankfurt: Peter Lang.

Atkinson, P. and Hammersley, M. (1998) Ethnography and participant observation. In N.K. Denzin and Y.S. Lincoln (eds) *Strategies of Qualitative Inquiry*. Thousand Oaks, CA: Sage.

Benson, P. (1996) *The multiple meanings of autonomy in language learning*. Paper given at Autonomy 2000, Bangkok.

Benson, P. and Lor, W. (1998) *Making Sense of Autonomous Language Learning*. English Centre Monograph, No.2. Hong Kong: The University of Hong Kong.

Connelly, F.M. and Clandinin, D.J. (1990) Stories of experience and narrative inquiry. *Educational Researcher*, 19,5:2-14.

Farmer, R. (1994) The limits of learner independence in Hong Kong. In Gardner, D. and Miller, L. (eds) *Directions in Self-Access Language Learning*. Hong Kong: Hong Kong University Press.

Harada, T. (1994) Gakusee no shuushoku to gakusee seekatsu ni kansuru ishiki choosa. *Shizuoka Daigaku Kyooiku Gakubu Jiko Tenken Hyooka Hookokusho*, 1993, 62-82.

The Asahi Shimbun (1993) *Haru ni sakanai puro no yume*. April 17.

Hata, T. et al. (1993) Shizuoka Daigaku kyooiku gakubusee no zaigaku ishiki ni kansuru choosa kenkyuu. *Shizuoka Daigaku Kyooiku Gakubu Fuzoku Kyooiku Jissenn Kenkyuu Shidoo Sentaa Kiyoo*, 2:203-32.

Ho, J. and Crookall, D. (1995) Breaking with Chinese cultural traditions: learner autonomy in English language teaching. *System*, 23,2:235-43.

Jones, J. (1995) Self-access and culture: retreating from autonomy. *ELT Journal*, 49,3:228-34.

Kvale, S. (1996) *InterViews: an introduction to qualitative research interviewing*. Thousand Oaks, CA: Sage.

Little, D. (1997) Strategies, counselling and cultural difference: why we need an anthropological understanding of learner autonomy. Paper given at the 6th Conference on Autonomous Learning, Barcelona.

Littlewood, W. (1999) Defining and developing autonomy in East Asian contexts. *Applied Linguistics*, 20,1:71-94.

Nedelsky, J. (1989) Reconceiving autonomy: Sources, thoughts and possibilities. *Yale Journal of Law and Feminism*, 1:7-36.

Pierson, H. D. (1996) Learner culture and learner autonomy in the Hong Kong Chinese context. In Pemberton, R., Li, E. S. L., Or, W. W. F. and Pierson, H. D. (eds) *Taking Control: Autonomy in Language Learning*. Hong Kong: Hong Kong University Press.

Riley, P. (1988) The ethnography of autonomy. In A. Brookes and P. Grundy (eds) *Individualization and Autonomy in Language Learning*. London: The British Council.

Rogers, C. R. (1980) *A Way of Being*. New York: Houghton Mifflin.

Ryan, R. M. (1991) The nature of the self in autonomy and relatedness. In J. Strauss and G. R. Goethal (eds) *The Self: interdisciplinary approaches*. New York: Springer-Verlag.

About the authors

David Crabbe, Alison Hoffmann and Sara Cotterall are involved in language teacher education, and the teaching of English for Academic Purposes and writing skills at Victoria University of Wellington. Each has research interests in learner autonomy. They are currently collaborating on a project aimed at exploring the quality of individual learning by language learners enrolled at Victoria University.

Richard Pemberton is a Senior Language Instructor and the Manager of the Self-Access Centre at the Hong Kong University of Science and Technology (HKUST). *Sarah Toogood, Susanna Ho and Jacqueline Lam* are Language Instructors in the Self-Access Centre at HKUST. All four have wide experience in running self-directed language learning programmes.

Beverly-Ann Carter is a Lecturer in French Language in the Department of Liberal Arts Faculty of Humanities and Education, University of the West Indies, St. Augustine. Her research on learner autonomy was the major focus of her Ph.D thesis, which she has completed with distinction.

Jose Lai is a Senior Instructor of the English Language Teaching Unit of The Chinese University of Hong Kong. Apart from conducting English courses for undergraduates, she also engages in teacher education and coordinates a course on developing learner autonomy in language learning. Her current research interests include learner autonomy, cooperative learning and programme evaluation.

The faculty of AIT's Center for Language and Educational Technology work with the Institute's Asia-wide student body on pre-masters, language and academic support, and research and writing programs. In addition, they also collaborate on educational development activities with other organisations and institutions in Southeast Asia.

Lienhard Legenhausen is Professor of Language Pedagogy at the University of Münster, Germany. His research interests include the study of learner language, technology-enhanced language learning (TELL) as well as learner-centred approaches to classroom learning/teaching.

Richard C. Smith was an Associate Professor at Tokyo University of Foreign Studies when he wrote the paper included in this volume. He is now lecturer in ELT and Applied Linguistics at the Centre for English Language Teacher Education, University of Warwick, UK.

Naoko Aoki teaches Japanese as a second-language teaching methodology at School of Letters, Osaka University, Japan. She has been interested in the concept of autonomy since she read *Deschooling Society* in the early 1970s.

Leni Dam, co-convenor and organiser of the symposium on learner autonomy in Tokyo in 1999, is an educational adviser and in-service teacher trainer at the Danish University of Education, Copenhagen, as well as a teacher of English in a Danish comprehensive school. She has been involved in innovation and research within education since 1976, especially the development of learner autonomy.

The AILA Review
Address all correspondence relating to the AILA Review to:
  David Graddol
  Managing Editor, AILA Review
  School of Education
  Open University
  Milton Keynes
  MK7 6AA, United Kingdom

  d.j.graddol@open.ac.uk